WHO KILLED...?
CLEVELAND, OHIO

BY: **JACK SWINT**

ROOFTOP
publishing

Rooftop Publishing™
1663 Liberty Drive, Suite 200
Bloomington, IN 47403
Phone: 1-800-839-8640

This book is a work of non-fiction. Unless otherwise noted, the author and the publisher make no explicit guarantees as to the accuracy of the information contained in this book and in some cases, names of people and places have been altered to protect their privacy.

First published by Rooftop Publishing 3/30/2007

ISBN: 978-1-60008-030-2 (sc)

Library of Congress Control Number: 2007924425

"Who Killed ...?" is a trademark of Rooftop Publishing

Printed in the United States of America
Bloomington, Indiana

This book is printed on acid-free paper.

A Tribute to Russell Elliott

The "Who Killed …?" series is a tribute to the memory of Russell Elliott of Bloomington, IN, who was murdered on April 7, 2004, and to all unsolved murder victims across our country who deserve to be recognized and their killers brought to justice. Should you have information about the Russell Elliott case, please contact Detective B.W. Smith at 317-367-1051.

Introduction

Since the days of Cain and Abel, people have murdered one another for various reasons. FBI statistics show that of the 16, 137 murders across the country in 2004, only 64 percent were solved, and out of that percentage, 70.2 percent have been committed by an acquaintance of the deceased. We will be examining some of the remaining percent of those untimely deaths that are to this date unsolved. Yes, it is a small percentage; nonetheless, it is a statistic that stands out as being the most intriguing number of murders that are committed. These are the most gruesome or heartbreaking of cases that society, families, and law enforcement are unable to forget.

As you read these fifteen cold-blooded cases, pay close attention to the facts outlined and other details being provided. We are not claiming to be able to solve any of these crimes; our only intent is to bring these murders back into the public's eye. With the passing of time, hopefully someone will come forward now with information helpful to close these cases and bring the guilty to justice.

Police agencies along with the victims' families are asking for your help in solving these crimes. Investigating officers' names and/or phone numbers are included at the closing of each story, and we urge you to call with any information that could be helpful in the arrest and conviction of the killers. You will also find our E-mail address along with a phone number if you would rather contact us directly, and the information will be passed along to the proper authorities.

This series of books begins in the Cleveland, Ohio, and surrounding areas, which hold fame to some of the most notorious and gruesome unsolved murders in the entire country. In fact, Cleveland itself holds one little known secret that was a blemish to one of our most famous lawmen in history. Federal Agent Eliot Ness had to finally concede to the defeat that he could not solve the most gruesome of multiple killings that he himself had ever investigated.

Authorities have claimed that these twelve victims could be the first serial killings known in Ohio or this region. And the fact that these gruesome murders occurred sixty-eight years ago and remain unsolved opens a possibility that the serial killer is still alive today.

It's here that we begin to unfold the truth, fact, and fiction of these unsolved murders by asking the question, "Who killed …?"

Contents

Who Was the Mad Butcher?

Cleveland, Ohio, in late 1935 was gearing up for the mayoral elections. Facing the incumbent was a city quickly growing tired of decades of police corruption, crooked politicians who all seemed to favor the Mob, bootleggers, and other crimes that could line their pockets with cash.

Elected on a campaign promise to clean up Cleveland once and for all, Republican Harold Burton meant to make good his word when he swiftly moved into office and hired former "G-Man" Eliot Ness, pictured below, as his chief of police and fire departments.

The good citizens of this city now had every reason to believe that crime and corruption were on the next train out of town. After only a short time on his new job, a call came in to the police station in the early morning hours of January 26th to say that parts of a human body were found lying against a building on East Twenty-first Street.

Upon investigating the claim, police found several dismembered body parts in a burlap bag and a bushel basket.

 After taking the lower half of a woman's torso, both thighs, and her right upper extremity to the coroner's office, it was determined that the woman had been dead several days and had been dismembered methodically with a very sharp instrument. Later, she was identified by fingerprint records as forty-two-year-old Flo Polillo. She had a police record for prostitution. Neighbors remember her as being very friendly, and she had had a previous marriage to a good husband before a divorce that led her to abusive beatings by sordid boyfriends.

Four months prior to this new grisly discovery, two teenage boys were playing in the field known as Kingsbury Run at the foot of Forty-ninth Street when they discovered two headless bodies lying naked and in severed pieces. It was determined that both men had been decapitated while still conscious since the muscles in their necks were retracted. One victim was identified as twenty-eight-year-old Edward Andrassy, whose last known address was 1744 Fulton Road in Cleveland. The other body was never identified and only noted as "victim #1." Mr. Andrassy was thought to have had several enemies who could have motive to kill him. Others thought he was just a "snotty punk kid" and even the police knew of him and had nothing favorable to say.

Up until this time, no one had even considered the possibility that this could be the work of a serial killer. The investigators hadn't thought or even suggested that there could be a connection to Flo Polillo or to a case a year earlier when the lower half of a woman's torso down to her knees had washed up onshore from Lake Erie by an amusement park. The remainder of her body was never discovered, and the police came to nickname her as

"The Lady of the Lake" or officially as "victim 0." Any leads on these murders soon dried up, and the police lost hope of solving the crimes.

Investigators during this time in history took a different approach to solving murders than they do today. In the 1930s, police were trained to just track down everyone with a motive until the killer was found. Today's forensic science and other modern technology methods were unheard of. Police relied solely on their training, instincts, a coroner's report, and their ideas and opinions.

It was now June of 1936, and except for the recent torso murders, the city was rebuilding as promised by the new mayor. Ness had overhauled the police department, and a major crackdown on organized crime had the press focusing on the positive changes being made in Cleveland. City officials were relaxed and making ready for the Republican National Convention due to begin in a few short days. Chief Ness was spending every waking hour preparing security plans for the candidates. He was well aware his career and reputation were on the line if anything went wrong over the next week of the convention.

The morning of June 5, 1936, brought with it the initial influx of delegates and other high-society Republicans for a week of political and social enjoyment. Only a few blocks away, two young teens set out to go fishing by taking a shortcut they knew through Kingsbury Run. One of the boys noticed a pair of pants under a bush out of the corner of his eye as they walked along. After poking at it with his fishing rod, a man's head rolled out and stopped right in between where both of them stood. Screaming and running at the same time, they both ended up together at one of their homes and waited there all day until an adult came home to tell their story to.

After a call was made to police, the area where the head was found was overtaken by law enforcement. Officers found the head, but it wasn't until the next morning that they found the naked decapitated remains in some bushes right in front of the Nickel Plate railroad police office. This victim was a tall slender man with distinctive and handsome features. Police thought that obtaining his identity would be easy since he had six distinctive tattoos on his body. It was speculated he may have been a sailor because of the cupid overlaying on an anchor. Another tattoo had the initials "W.C.G."; he also had others that displayed an arrow through a heart, the words "Helen-Paul," and assorted flags. His identity was never known, even after his body was put on display for people to view in hopes of learning who he was.

His body was found in an area known as "hobo country," but due to his neat appearance and the expensive clothing found near his body, speculation leaned towards his decapitated body having been dumped in this area. As with the other murders so far, the body had been drained of blood and washed clean before being dumped.

By that Sunday, the headlines and talk of the city had switched from the convention to the psycho killer who was chopping off the heads of people at his will and even under the nose of the police in an almost taunting manner. Eliot Ness had previously left the murders to his homicide division, but now there was a cry from the public to catch the killer or killers. He would have to become personally involved and utilize his own experience and training to solve these bizarre murders.

The chief met with his lead homicide detective Sergeant James Hogan and members of the crime lab to begin evaluating the recent murders and the facts that they knew at the time. Hogan so far had felt that these crimes were not all carried out by the same person. Ness concluded though that they all had been at the hands of one man. He was adamant about this being a one-man murder spree, and none of his subordinates dared to differ with him. The chief made it clear though not to tell the press they were searching for just one maniac and to keep their investigation private to just this small group. At least until the convention was over.

While still working on the case of the tattooed man, another call came in on July 22, 1936, claiming another murder had occurred. Police discovered the headless decomposed body of a white male lying on his stomach in the Big Creek area, which was home to a group of hobos. Conducting a search, they found his head near some clothes heaped in a pile not far away. This time, the coroner ruled that the remains had been there for approximately two months and that blood had drained from the body and soaked into the ground, which showed he had been killed right there unlike the previous bodies, which were drained of blood and cleaned before disposal.

Regardless, everyone investigating these deaths soon came to realize that Eliot Ness was correct in his assumption that this was the work of one madman and they had to act quickly to catch him. Keeping a low profile on this case was a top priority since the City of Cleveland had not only hosted the National Republican Convention, it was also home to the Great Lakes Expo each year and after that, the American Legion Convention to close out the summer. Outside of a cold trail of decapitated men and women, the city appeared to have the potential to become a bustling host to conventions and other attractions to earn a positive reputation for a change.

Just as the legionaries were about to arrive, Cleveland was once again snapped back to reality as another gruesome murder was discovered on September 10th near East Thirty-seventh Street in the form of two halves of a human torso floating in the water. As police and rescue workers searched the water and nearby weeds, they were able to find several other parts of a body and began fitting them together like a jigsaw puzzle. Chief Ness was visibly irritated as it became evident they had no solid leads or clues to this invisible and at-will psychopath's profile except that he could elude any attempts to be caught.

Meetings were held daily now about any progress being made. Finally after months of exhaustive man-hours, the police finally came up with a profile of the killer and other details that hopefully would lead them to a suspect. It was ruled out right away that the killer could be a woman because they felt she would not be able to make the deep cutting slices needed to sever a human body or be able to move the torsos around as freely as the killer had been able to do so far. While it was also clear this man was not entirely insane, the police thought that he must have psychopathic tendencies as well as a great deal of knowledge in regards to anatomy and/or the medical profession, like a surgeon would. Doctors argued that the same could be said for a hunter or butcher who also had the knowledge to commit this type of dissecting.

There was a disagreement over whether or not he was homosexual even though some of the corpses had their genitals cut off. They all agreed he was a very large and strong man and most likely acting alone. Victims were selected by social standing as being lowlifes, transients, or other undesirables. Most important was that this man had to have a private place where he could murder these people because of the bloody mess that would occur when decapitating a person while still alive— somewhere a person could be lured to also hide any screams or other gruesome sounds that each victim must have made.

Money and resources were not an issue to putting a stop to these killings. Chief Ness said to spare no costs or available officers. Police began searching out anyone with a mental condition by searching hospital records and interviewing suspects around the clock in what now had become four years of clueless homicides dating back to the Lady of the Lake in the early 1930s. Her death now was thought to be included in this one-man killing spree. One suspect was said to have walked the streets at night with a large butcher knife. Then there was the man nicknamed "the chicken freak" because he enjoyed hiring prostitutes to sit naked in front of him while they beheaded live chickens as he masturbated. One was a proclaimed voodoo doctor, and the list went on and on into the hundreds of people interviewed, which turned up nothing. It appeared that everyone in Cleveland knew the identity of the killer, but the countless tips received by the police always turned up empty.

By the end of the year, Ness and his men were no closer to solving the serial killings than when they began their investigation. Hope of 1937 bringing a reprieve from the madman was quickly diminished with the discovery of three more decapitated bodies who became known only as victims seven, eight, and nine because police had no more of an idea who these victims were than the others. The first occurred in February when a headless torso washed up on the shores at 156th Street. The last of the three occurred in September 1937 and left law enforcement once again chasing their tails. Except for being able to identify Edward Andrassy and Flo Polillo, the police never knew the names of the remaining victims. It was as if the killer now made sure no one could put a name to his prey.

The murder of July 1937 bore all of the killer's traits, except this time all of the dead woman's internal organs had been removed as well. Ness and the coroner both felt this was significant as being the signature of a surgeon. Police now began to focus all of their attention on physicians, medical students, and male nurses. Surveillance was set in place to keep a close watch on doctors who had any history of sexual misconduct, alcohol or drug abuse, and even known homosexual activity.

A potential break came when police identified physician Frank E. Sweeney, who seemed to fit the profile. A tall man with a large build, he was visually a strong man who had grown up in the Kingsbury Run area, where many of the murders occurred. His office was also located there, which gave officers more reason to suspect him. The doctor reportedly had a serious drinking problem, which caused his divorce, and rumors were alleged that he had a violent temper and had bisexual tendencies.

Investigators found two disturbing facts surrounding the theory that the doctor was their man. Records showed him to be in the veterans' hospital in Sandusky, Ohio, at the time of at least two murders, and he was the first cousin of U.S. Congressman Martin Sweeney, who was very outspoken as a critic of Cleveland's mayor and Chief Eliot Ness.

Democrat Congressman Sweeney felt that both the mayor and Ness were spending all of their time and money trying to prosecute crooked cops from the bootlegging era instead of solving the important issues like the multiple killings of the maniac on the loose. Doctor Sweeney was soon ruled out as a suspect by most of the detectives, so the police picked up where they had left off with no clues or ideas of who the real killer was.

In March of 1938, in Sandusky, Ohio, a dog retrieved the leg of a man lying in a swampy area outside of town. Lt. Cowles of the Cleveland Police Department personally went there in hopes of finding evidence that this murder was connected to the serial killer. His hopes were soon squashed when it was determined the leg was not of a murdered person—instead, it was from a patient at the hospital who had had his leg amputated. On a hunch though, Lt. Cowles recalled that Dr. Sweeney had been a patient at this same veterans' hospital, so he decided to interview some of the staff there about the physician's frequent visits that coincided with some of the murders in Cleveland.

What the detective learned from his interviews placed Sweeney back at the top of the list of suspects and in the mind of the veteran officer nailed this suspect down to being the murderer. It appeared that the good doctor was only there on a voluntary basis and that he could basically come and go at will. Checking the dates closely, Cowles found that Sweeney had indeed been in the hospital, but with Cleveland only two hours away, he could have driven or hopped a train and committed the murders and made it back to Sandusky before anyone was the wiser.

Upon his return, a quiet but intense surveillance was conducted on the doctor day to day. At times, following him was blatant, and the police did not care if the suspect knew it because if nothing else it might stop him from committing another murder. Interviewing his family members gave them more information; apparently, alcoholism and even psychosis ran in his family. Eliot Ness now felt they had their man and it was just a matter of time before they could bring him in for questioning. Of course, it would be done discreetly if possible so as not to alert the media or the U.S. congressman that his relative was a suspect for the same murders that the politician was so vocal about the police being unable to solve.

Before Ness could move on his notions, in April of 1938 police were notified that a female leg had been fished from the Cuyahoga River. The chief stated his belief was that these findings were nothing more than remains from a local hospital, boating accident, or anything other than a new murder. His hopes were gone when the coroner ruled that the leg found was only a few days old, and one month later, her decapitated torso was also found washed up onshore. Surveillance on Sweeney was now around the clock; they searched his office and even checked his mail.

When public outcry was just starting to subside from the latest killing, pieces of another body surfaced at a dump on East Ninth Street. Scavengers searching through the junk and debris found the woman's body wrapped in rags and covered with cardboard. Unlike the others, her hands and head were also alongside the rest of the remains. While they were combing the area for more evidence, someone found more bones and a skull lodged inside a tin can.

One fingerprint discovered on the woman's hand was printable, but police were never able to match it with any records. Both of these new corpses' identities would also remain unknown except for their place in line with the others as "victims 11 and 12." Lt. Cowles never accepted the idea that these two were victims of the mad butcher because of the variance in the unprofessional severing of their body parts and the fact that this murderer left the hands and head of the woman with the torso. This killer appeared to hide the bodies in a dump unlike the others where the serial killer wanted someone to find his victims. As far as he was concerned, this must be a separate incident.

Due to the intense scrutiny he and the department were receiving from the public, Ness was forced into a desperate move to solve this case. He arranged for a secret meeting with and interrogation of Dr. Sweeney. Not wanting to alarm the press or the congressman, they met in a suite at the Cleveland Hotel on August 23, 1938. Ness brought with him a court psychiatrist,

Lt. Cowles, and Dr. Leonard Keeler, who helped invent the polygraph. By the end of the meeting and polygraph tests, all four men believed that Doctor Frank Sweeney was their man. The chief admitted—though he found it very hard to believe after talking to Sweeney—that this well-educated, professional person could be that maniac butcher they were after.

There was no solid evidence though to arrest, much less convict this man. All they had to go on were their beliefs. Tightening down to twenty-four-hour/seven-day surveillance would not do much good either since Sweeney had proven he could elude a tail if he wanted to.

A strange chain of events occurred shortly after their meeting. Frank Sweeney admitted himself into the Sandusky veterans' hospital on August 25, 1938, and transferred back and forth between there and other hospitals until his death in 1965. Like his prior hospitalization, he could come and go pretty much as he pleased.

During this time, serial killings in other states had similarities on the surface, but nothing concrete ever linked them together. The murders in Cleveland officially stopped in 1938; the search for the killer is still open today. Other suspects were identified and even arrested by the local sheriff. Frank Dolezal, who had only frequented the same bar as both Andrassy and Polillo before their deaths, became a prime target. It was a far stretch of the imagination to believe that Dolezal was the mad butcher just because he had visited the same bar as the first victims, but the sheriff wanted to solve the case. It is reported that after intense and possibly brutal long hours of interrogations, the man broke down and signed a confession for the murder of Flo Polillo.

The interrogation and confession were not conducted by the Cleveland police. Sheriff Martin O'Donnell, longtime ally of Congressman Sweeney and family, made the arrest on July 5, 1939. The Cleveland city police detectives were never told beforehand of the sheriff's involvement or the arrest of Dolezal.

This bizarre, gruesome, and unsolved murder spree has never been resolved. Was Doctor Frank Sweeney the mad butcher? The killings appeared to stop in 1938 when he admitted himself into the hospital. Coincidence, or did Sweeney's hospitalization provide the opportune time for the real killer to safely leave Cleveland and then resurface in another city? Some have said they don't believe all of the twelve murders were done by the same person. Even though all were decapitated, some bodies were mutilated differently than the rest, as though someone else had either tried to copy the real murderer or cover his or her own crime.

In December 1939, an anonymous letter was sent from California to Cleveland Police Chief George Matowitz. It started, "You can rest easy now, as I have come out to sunny California for the winter. I felt bad operating on those people, but science must advance." The typed letter continues: "What did their lives mean in comparison to hundreds of sick and disease twisted bodies? Just laboratory guinea pigs found on any public street. No one missed them when I failed. My last case was successful. I know now the feeling of Pasteur, Thoreau and other pioneers."

An editorial in the *Cleveland News* in 1936:

> He kills for the thrill of killing. He kills to satisfy a bestial, sadistic lust for blood. He kills to prove himself strong. He kills to feed his sex-perverted brain, the sight of a beheaded human. He must kill for decapitation is his drug, to be taken in closer-spaced doses. Yes he will kill again. He is of course insane.

In August of 2000, haunting memories of the torso murders resurfaced again when another two Cleveland boys discovered a torso in a vacant East Side lot. These two youths were walking home from swimming when they came upon the dismembered body near East Ninety-first Street. Identical to the 1930s' decapitation and systematic dissecting, the remains were believed to have been dumped there after being murdered somewhere else. Ironically, the discovery was only a short distance from Kingsbury Run.

Just like in the thirties, police were baffled and could not discover a suspect or the identity of the torso. According to the coroner's report, this was a white male about twenty-two years old. He had a tattoo on his left shoulder of a red flower with green leaves. Above the flower is the name "Natasha." There was another tattoo of a Puerto Rican flag with a heart next to it. All of this leads to the questions: Is it possible that the same mental disease that drove the original killer is alive today in one of his children? Or is this just the work of a copycat murderer?

There aren't many clues, suspects, or facts to go on except at least twelve people lost their heads to the maniac police called the "Mad Butcher" of Cleveland.

Doctor Frank Sweeney was never charged, arrested, or tried for these crimes. He was only identified and investigated as a suspect in these killings.

Research and development of this story was made possible with the help of the Cleveland Police Department and Cleveland Public Library, along with published stories in the *Plain Dealer* newspaper and Court TV's "Crime Library."

Who Strangled and Killed Seven Women of Cleveland?

In 1994, George Forbes, president of the Cleveland NAACP, voiced his opinion that he felt a person's class in society played an important role in how crimes were prioritized by both the media and law enforcement—that lower-class adults, not just blacks, received less importance and public notice than middle- and upper-class citizens. Yvonne Pointer, a strong advocate for the families of the victims of violent crimes and a liaison with the Ohio Attorney General's Office, says the criminal justice system provides fewer resources to investigate crimes against poor black women. Her own fourteen-year-old daughter was murdered in 1984, and the crime still goes unsolved today.

In 1993 alone, five women were strangled and killed in the first seven months, and two more were strangled in the first three months of 1994. Was this a serial killer on the loose? Opinions were divided, even in law enforcement. Local police never called in the FBI because they felt there was no real evidence to connect all the crimes. Even

Cuyahoga County Coroner Elizabeth Balraj said she did not notice any similarities or any evidence to link the strangulations.

The Cleveland *Plain Dealer* asked retired FBI agent Robert Ressler, who coincidently was one of the key persons who helped set up the Bureau's Behavior Science Unit, which aids police, if he felt the strangulations were connected. His answer: "The possibility is obvious; it's something that needs to be looked at." A professor of psychiatric mental health for the University of Pennsylvania agreed with Ressler. Ann Burgess said the strangulations "point to at least several victims being connected to one possible suspect."

What are the odds that seven women could be strangled to death in just a little over a year by seven different assailants? Not to mention the reports from several other women who claimed that they were strangled by a man and luckily escaped before being killed. And do murder investigations become "profiled" by a person's social standing in this country? All seven women were either strippers or prostitutes. Did the news media pick and choose what brings in ratings so they can sensationalize? Media does have the power to direct pressure when exposing crime. Or was it that authorities never asked for the media's help? Today in Cleveland, for example, news bureau Channel 19 gets very up-close and personal and exposes anything and everything that needs public knowledge, even if it takes knocking on doors or hiding in the bushes. No racial or social boundaries or government red tape hold them back from reporting the news. Or is it just that we as a society rate lives years ago and even today as Yvonne Pointer and George Forbes allege?

Regardless, the real reason these young women were murdered on the streets of Cleveland is not relevant. Their deaths have not been solved. There has been no closure for the victims or their families. If they are related as serial killings, then he is still a free man and able to kill again. Today's modern technology may be able to answer that question if authorities reopen these unsolved murders.

Through research of these ladies' lives from available news and other records, this is the only information that was made available to the public at that time.

1) Lakeitha Chapman was twenty-eight years old when she was strangled to death on January 29, 1993. Lakeitha was found in a parking lot off East Ninety-ninth Street. Josephine Jordan, Lakeitha's mother, said, "Men would jump on her and beat her; they'd make her go out and make money." Her mother went on to say that her daughter was drawn to the streets in 1988 or 1989. "Finally I prayed and put it in the hands of God." There was a one-line sentence about her murder in the *Plain Dealer* in January 1993 and then in April of 1994. No other information was made available to the public.

2) Gloria Pennington was found strangled to death on February 8, 1993, in an abandoned building on Russell Avenue. There was no mention of her murder in 1993 in either the *Plain Dealer* or TV news. Nothing was told of her murder until April 1994 in the newspaper. No other information was made available to the public.

3) Tracey Hayes, twenty-three, was strangled to death on April 2, 1993, outside of Garfield Heights grocery store. There was no mention of her murder in 1993 in either the *Plain Dealer* or TV news. Nothing was told of her murder until April 1994 in the newspaper. No other information was made available to the public.

4) Darlene Nash, twenty-four, was found strangled to death on April 9, 1993, at East 106th Street and Union Avenue. Her mother, Lonnie, said in a 1994 interview she hadn't had a decent night's sleep since Darlene's body had been found. She left behind a daughter, Tyisha, who was then three years old and couldn't understand what happened to her mother. At eleven, Tyisha, according to Lonnie, often had nightmares and was often teased at school because she did not have a mother. There was a four-line article in the *Plain Dealer* on April 10, 1993, and then again in April 1994. No other information was made available to the public.

5) Shynicka Chatton, eighteen, was strangled to death on July 12, 1993, and found on East Eighty-eighth Street. There was no mention of her murder in 1993 in either the *Plain Dealer* or TV news. Nothing was told of her murder until April 1994 in the newspaper. No other information was made available to the public.

6) Rotunda Baker, twenty-six, was strangled to death on February 22, 1994, and her body was found at East 166th Street and St. Clair Avenue. There was no mention of her murder in February of 1994 in either the *Plain Dealer* or TV news. Nothing was told of her murder until April 1994 in the newspaper. No other information was made available to the public.

7) Emma Jackson, thirty-five, was strangled to death on March 25, 1994, and her body was found at East 101st Street and Cedar Avenue. There was one article in the *Plain Dealer* in March of 1994 and another one in April of 1994. No other information was made available to the public.

During this same time period, "Project Second Chance" counselors Sondra Collins and Theresa Maddaleana told news sources that they'd had prostitutes tell them about encounters with a man who attempted to strangle them. Both said that in 1993 and 1994 they believed someone was killing prostitutes in Cleveland. A forty-six-year-old prostitute told Maddaleana that a man took her to Sixty-eighth Street near Cedar Avenue and tried to strangle her. Lanett Sellers, then twenty-four and enrolled in the Second Chance program, told counselors she was assaulted by a "chubby man" who took her to the West Technical High School and tried to choke her twice.

Sellers stated that she doesn't know how she escaped but she "put up a hell of a fight." She also said that she will never be able to forget the man's face. "It was like a look I'd never seen before. He looked like the devil to me."

Dellmus Colvin, pictured to the left, a Toledo, Ohio, trucker, confessed to at least five murders of Toledo area prostitutes back in 2003. He later admitted to more killings dating back to at least 2000. Police also contacted more than one hundred other law enforcement agencies across the country to inquire of other truck driver-type serial killings. One was the 1996 murder of exotic dancer Victoria Collins of Cleveland, which Colvin confessed to. In 1994, 139 people were murdered in the city of Cleveland. Police solved 73 percent of the cases, and in most, convictions were obtained.

Police still ask for your help with these unsolved murder cases. They have said not to discount the relevance of any information you may know. Your piece of information may have a significant impact on the investigation when viewed in the context of what they already know.

For further information, call 216-621-1234, or you can E-mail Unsolvedmurder07@aol.com, and we will pass along this information.

Research and development of this story was made possible by the assistance of the Cleveland Public Library, *Plain Dealer* newspaper, Cleveland Police reports, and friends and family of these victims.

Who Killed Tammy Beetler of Lorain, Ohio?

As a lot of people across the country were glued to their TVs watching the O.J. Simpson trial on Friday, February 10, 1995, thirty-one-year-old Tammy Beetler was returning home from walking to the grocery store. It  was a typical busy morning that started the day with getting her two kids off to school. Husband Dale had been working for several hours and wouldn't be home from his job at ServPro until 5 p.m. This would be her time to relax before eleven-year-old William and nine-year-old Amanda returned home in the afternoon. Neighbors described the Beetlers, pictured above, as quiet and nice people living in a working-class neighborhood for the last ten years. It had been at least a year since reported drug activity kept a steady traffic of people on the neighborhood streets.

Tammy walked into her house, located at 404 West Twenty-first Street in Lorain, Ohio, with the groceries she had purchased and closed the door behind her. Sometime around 12:30 p.m., one of the neighbors recalls hearing dogs barking, which caught his attention due to the loud continuous commotion they were making. He wasn't sure exactly where they were, but it was close by and in the direction of Tammy's residence. The Beetlers owned two dogs that were kept in the backyard. Later when the children came home from school, they found the front door locked, so both went around the corner to Lexington Avenue, where their grandmother lived, to wait for their mom to come home.

A short time later, around 4:50 p.m., Dale Beetler was arriving home from work as he noticed his two kids and his mother, Dolores, approaching the house. As they all entered the home, everything appeared to be normal except Tammy was not answering her kids' or husband's calls out to her. Within a few minutes, police dispatchers were answering a frantic 911 call from the Beetler residence to please send help; someone was dead. The kids had discovered their mother's body in her bedroom on the floor still dressed but in a pool of blood.

When police and paramedics arrived, they found Mrs. Beetler dead. She had severe gash-type wounds that the coroner later described as being caused by "considerable force." She had suffered a total of forty-six separate blows; some appeared to be from something sharp and others from a blunt object. The coroner, Paul Matus, stated that she either died of severe head and brain trauma or a serious chest injury. "Take your pick," the coroner stated. "Either one can kill a person." Detectives began working sixteen-hour days following the discovery of her battered body and felt they were developing positive leads and expecting something to break soon. The Ohio Bureau of Investigation sent their team of experts immediately to the murder scene and requested that the home be secured and the body not removed until they also could examine the evidence.

Rumors quickly spread like wildfire by West Twenty-first Street neighbors and others in town when they learned of the murder in Elyria, Ohio, of seventy-nine-year-old Russell Reedy just five days after Tammy was killed. Lorain was only eight minutes from Reedy's hometown, and speculation now was that the two cases might be related. The murder in Elyria was discovered to be at the hands of a seventeen-year-old mental patient from the Nord Center, a hospital and rehabilitation facility that has provided mental health services to the residents of Lorain County since 1948. Police ruled out a patient committing this murder and focused more on the coming and going of visitors to the Beetler home.

Detectives along with an FBI profiler felt that the killer was someone known by Tammy and/or Dale, a person whom she must have felt comfortable with if she had possibly opened the door to him. There was no sign of a forced entry, and nothing was missing from their home, ruling out a robbery. Neither was there any evidence that she had been sexually assaulted. Reports indicated the Beetlers had a lot of acquaintances who were seen visiting them in age ranges from seventeen to thirty years old. On February 12, investigators made a public plea for the community's help across news media in hopes of new evidence, suspects, and/or leads. A $1,000 reward for information leading to an arrest and conviction was also offered.

At least eight tips came into the detective bureau from their request for help from the public. Then Lorain police captain John Reiber said he was very pleased with the response from concerned citizens who wanted to help. He felt that most of the calls came from tipsters who did not even realize there was a reward. "I think some people were just coming forward on their own." Reiber continued in a news interview stating, "Nothing solid came up, and we're still not ready to make an arrest." The captain assured everyone that they would investigate every lead and possible motive to solve this murder.

Dale Beetler had been temporarily ruled out as a primary suspect after being interviewed. They hadn't ruled out domestic violence, but Dale had been at work the afternoon his wife was murdered. Detectives contended Beetler was being cooperative and assisting the police in their investigation.

Mr. Beetler was visibly shaken and distraught at the loss of his wife. His mother described the children's and her son's conditions to the *Morning Journal* newspaper in Lorain as very distraught and lost without their mother and wife. "My son worked and lived for her and those kids," Dolores said. "He's not doing good at all." Tammy's mother-in-law described her as being the best she could have ever hoped for and that she couldn't have found anyone any sweeter than Dale's wife. Mrs. Beetler was a stay-at-home mother for her children and was often seen walking both kids to Hawthorne Elementary. In fact, she did not drive and walked everywhere she needed to go when not with her husband as he drove.

Dorothy Summers, Tammy's mother, who lived in Florence Township, Ohio, had always hoped her daughter and Dale would pack up and move away from where they lived in Lorain. She said she was scared of a crime occurring where they lived with her grandchildren. Mrs. Summers never felt that Tammy and Dale's neighborhood was a good environment for their kids to grow up in. Even the staff where the kids attended school remember Mrs. Beetler as a dedicated mother who always volunteered to help out when they needed her.

Tammy was the youngest of four children, with older brothers Doug and Larry and older sister Margie. Everett Summers, the kids' father, was deceased. Tammy had quit going to Firelands High School a year before her graduation to marry her first husband, Peter Neal. After five years of marriage, they divorced, and Tammy became a single mom with the couple's son, William. After meeting Dale Beetler sometime later, the couple married and had their daughter, Amanda. Tammy did go back and get her GED but never went to work. As most people know though, raising kids is a job. "She was a good mother and loved her children very much."

The trauma from discovering the body of their mother will always be a haunting memory in William and Amanda's lives. It's unimaginable to be so young and to find anyone, much less a parent, murdered in cold blood. One of Tammy's friends, Debra Arnett, volunteered out of pure love and concern for William and Amanda to try to help them cope with the loss of their mother. Their grandmother also spent time trying to answer questions and alleviate fears that the killer may even come back for them. Amanda wanted to sleep with a fingernail file under her pillow for protection. William cried a lot, and like his father, he was just lost without his mom.

Either through total desperation or a feeling of helplessness and determination to catch the murderer, Dale began to investigate his own wife's death. "The killer took my world away from me," he explained to the local newspaper. Mr. Beetler said he felt that the police were not following up on his tips to them and that he had people out asking questions because the police were moving too slowly. Even though officers felt it was a slap in the face and were bewildered by Dale's comments to the press, they also understood the frustration and pain he was enduring from the death of his wife.

As with all investigations, more so murder, the police could not provide Dale or anyone else with a minute-by-minute status on the twelve to fourteen hours a day following leads and talking to suspects. Nor would they elaborate to anyone outside of law enforcement on the direction of their investigation. And during this time, Dale and some of his friends had not been ruled out totally as suspects. In reality, Beetler may have hindered the police by having his associates and himself digging into his wife's murder. As then captain Reiber noted, they were waiting on reports from the labs and most of his available men were spending each day working on this case. "It's frustrating, but we have to have evidence before we take any action."

Three months passed by before police commented in April that they did indeed have "a couple or three really good suspects" according to Captain Reiber. Without naming any of the people they were considering, the captain stated, "It could be five minutes from now or never" when they would be able to make an arrest. It would be another eight months as the mystery of Tammy's murder would cause the police to raise the reward to $5,000 in hopes of sparking new leads. Dale's mother was feeling the same total frustration as investigators when she received no calls or responses from all of the flyers and signs she had been posting about the reward and unsolved murder. Some people who saw the signs stated they thought the case had already been solved.

Lorain investigators were not about to allow dust to settle on this unsolved murder so they decided to hire an outside consulting company known for its "detection of deception" techniques according to the company's owner, Joseph Buckley. John Reid and Associates aid police departments all over the country, and by the time their two-day trip to Lorain was over, the police felt they had a new direction and fresh ideas toward the investigation of this murder. Police Chief Cel Rivera said that "when you're talking about such a brutal, cruel and vicious death it's not unusual to use any method that may help."

Dolores Beetler heard of the hiring of an outside agency and felt it was a positive move on the part of the police, and it renewed her spirits that they were still after Tammy's killer. She had taken custody of William and Amanda and was raising them herself. Investigator Rich Resendez said that the private company's expertise was helpful in ruling out some suspects, and based on recommendations from Reid and Associates, officers were now going to have evidence originally taken from the scene tested for DNA samples.

One year later, on the anniversary month of his wife's murder, Dale Beetler was arrested by Lorain police for carrying a concealed weapon and possession of a drug scale and rolling papers in his pocket. He also faced charges of reckless operation and aggravated menacing. He reportedly pulled a gun on police and then ran into a home on West Twenty-eighth Street. Beetler explained that he had carried the gun for protection since his wife was murdered. People interviewed say they weren't sure why he would need to carry a gun unless he felt the murderer was after him as well. But that did not explain the scales and rolling papers.

Moving forward in time to December 2006, the Lorain Detective Bureau is under the leadership of Captain Cambarare. Utilizing new technology and CSI training, his officers have in a sense gone back in time and brought several cold case murders up to date with modern technical skills. There has been a world of change going on in police work since the murder of Tammy Beetler. At the time in 1995, officers may have been thinking and planning ahead when they seized certain evidence for future use. And Captain Cambarare feels confident that time is now.

Assigning Detective Edward Bermudez of the Criminal Investigation Bureau (pictured to the right with Captain Cambarare) to head up the Beetler case brings a set of new goals to solving her murder. When asked what level  of degree he places her case on his daily list of things to do, the detective summed it up with two swift words: "High priority." Not revealing his plan, Bermudez would say that he is going to utilize DNA evidence and his own crime scene experience to begin. One important thing, he says, is "re-interview all of the principal parties in this case and find new sources of information as well." Listening to Bermudez explain what he is allowed to discuss about Tammy's murder investigation, it is plain to see the detective is definitely geared up for it.

Lorain police won't come out openly and say, but there is a feeling they may have formulated a solid motive as to what caused the killer to attack her. If that is true, Bermudez and Cambarare are keeping that information close to themselves. He also said they are offering a $2,000 reward for information that will lead to an arrest and conviction of whoever killed Mrs. Beetler.

As with most cold cases, time has proven to help solve these types of crimes. Over a period of time, witnesses tend to feel more relaxed from any intimidation from a suspect from years ago and may be open to talk. And after so much time has elapsed, it is harder for the killer not to tell someone what he or she has done.

Police need your help in solving the murder of Tammy Beetler. They have said not to discount the relevance of any information you may know. Your piece of information may have a significant impact on the investigation when viewed in the context of what they already know.

For further information, contact Detective Edward Bermudez at (440) 204-2105, ext 234, or E-mail Ed_Bermudez@cityoflorain.org.

Research and development of this story was assisted by the Lorain City Police Department, the *Plain Dealer* and also the Reference Department, family and friends of Tammy and Dale Beetler, and the Lorain City Public Library.

Who Killed Amy Mihaljevic?

Amy Mihaljevic talked to her best friend Kristen Balas on Friday morning about the recent school picture that ten-year-old Amy was unhappy with. She couldn't wait until picture makeup day. That Friday, October 27, 1989, would not be a routine school day due to an assembly she and the other students would attend at the high school. Later, Amy and the rest of her classmates were visited by Police Officer Mark Spaetzel, whose part of the job being the rookie patrolman was to talk with the students about "child safety."

Fifth-graders were always released first at the end of the day. Kristen was a year ahead of her friend in school, so seeing Amy's blue and white bicycle still in the bike rack was unusual but not alarming. Figuring she had a doctor's appointment, the older girl headed on for home.

There is a belief that it is safer to live, work, or play close to a police department. It just makes sense because what criminal in his or her right mind would dare commit a crime so close to where the cops are stationed? Being safe wasn't the feeling at all for the ten-year-old this day. Why would she have a need to feel worried or afraid? Amy was excitedly happy because, according to the voice on the other end of the phone call a few days earlier, she was going to secretly help pick out a present for her mom's recent promotion at work. The unknown caller would also let Amy pick out a gift for herself.

She probably didn't care that the Bay Village, Ohio, police department was directly across the street from the plaza where she had walked to from school. Neither did the person she met that afternoon, as he must have sat in his vehicle and waited for the youngster to meet him. No one will ever know if she bought her mother a present that day; Amy was not heard from or seen again until four months later when a jogger found her lifeless body dumped fifty-two miles away in Ashland County, Ohio, on County Road 1181.

A mother's intuition and bond to her children sometimes leads to knowing when something just isn't right. So when Amy unexpectedly called her mother at work to say she was at choir tryouts after school, Margaret Mihaljevic felt something just wasn't right. A phone call that seemed hurriedly made by Amy confused her mother enough to trigger that instinct alarm. Mrs. Mihaljevic left work early that day to go home to check on her daughter. When Amy wasn't there, she knew something was wrong and headed out to the school, where she discovered Amy's bicycle still parked. She went straight to the police station to report her missing. Frantic searches to her friends' homes and phone calls to anyone she thought might know her daughter's whereabouts turned up nothing.

If Amy had already been kidnapped, why would she be allowed to call her mother at work? Was her abductor wanting to learn if anyone had witnessed her being taken from the plaza?

To find out if the police were already searching for her? Had witnesses given a description of the vehicle and person she had left with? If so, that was a clever move on her abductor's part to check if Amy's mother already knew something was wrong. Or had the little girl insisted she needed to call her mother, and he did so as not to cause Amy to become afraid in the beginning for her own safety?

If this killer was clever enough to prearrange the phone call that lured her to the plaza, and then had Amy call her mother at work, he surely had a contingency backup plan. If she did not know her abductor, he could then let her go and speed away. Had Amy known his identity, he could easily just take her to buy that gift for the mother and one for Amy as promised, then drive back to the school, let her get the bicycle, and if ever questioned by police claim it was a harmless misunderstanding.

Hours later, when it was apparent the little girl was missing, the police did in fact cordon off the town of Bay Village and the surrounding areas. The FBI was immediately called in, and volunteers began to gather and search everywhere they could to bring the ten-year-old home. Her father and a friend searched each street and even the creek beds, hoping Amy had just been out playing with friends and lost track of time. Anything except the reality his daughter may have been abducted.

Several witnesses came forward and told authorities they had seen Amy after school around 2:40 p.m. at the shopping center standing in front of the Baskin-Robbins Ice Cream Parlor. A clean-cut man, allegedly dressed in khaki trousers, a polo-type shirt, and what appeared to be a designer lightweight jacket, walked up to her and they both walked off together. At the time, reports of a van and/or truck in color shades of green to black were also described.

The FBI set up one command post in the basement of the police department, while the local citizens set up their own center on the first floor. Thousands of flyers with Amy's picture and information would be distributed throughout this region of Ohio from Cleveland to Ashland and beyond. Ohio TV stations began airing stories the first night about the abduction, and talk of the beautiful missing ten-year-old was on the minds and lips of everyone. Bay Village residents and law enforcement would work around the clock. Everyone was determined to bring Amy home alive. Volunteers came from all walks of life, and tips were being phoned in by the hundreds of possible suspects, sightings, and well-wishing people hoping for the best.

Years earlier, residents of Bay Village, Ohio, had been the focus of another high-profile crime. On July 4, 1954, Marilyn Sheppard, wife of Doctor Samuel Sheppard, was murdered in her home in this same town. The doctor was convicted for the murder, then later acquitted, and the story became sensationalized in the TV series and movie *The Fugitive*. Now thirty-five years later, another criminal act would spotlight the area again.

The FBI began following up on leads they felt were the most promising. By the time the investigation was into its ninth month, their search had taken every twist and turn conceivable. Potential suspects from family to friends were interviewed and hundreds of leads were narrowed down to at least five men who became the focal points and prime targets for the murder. To this date, no arrests have been made even though police contend they are still investigating any leads and will make an arrest someday.

To focus on the alleged prime suspects identified to date, we will turn back to the last day Amy was seen alive. According to written reports and witnesses, she rode her bike to the home of best friend Kristen Balas, which was a ritual for the two girls. They pedaled to school, and Amy was in Mrs. Stewart's class before the 7:50 a.m. bell. Another friend, Kristy Sabo, recalls seeing her in class as Kristy walked by after lunch. Class for the fifth-graders let out at 2:10 p.m., and instead of picking up her bike, Amy left it behind and walked.

Student Olivia Masiak walked with Amy towards the plaza and asked her why she was going that way instead of riding her bike home. Amy allegedly said she was "meeting a friend." Others also said that she had told them about the phone call days earlier asking her to meet someone after school Friday to help buy a present for Amy's mother's recent work promotion. (It was revealed years later that other girls in town reported getting the same type of phone calls from a man with the same scenario. None of them took the caller up on his offer.) Another girl, Haley Pritchard, said she was walking behind Amy when she saw her stroll over to a black van but then head over to the Baskin-Robbins store.

Most Bay Village police officers were across the street from Amy during this time for a meeting inside the police department. At approximately 2:30 p.m., a group of older kids who had skipped class were standing nearby as they eyed a police cruiser pulling onto the lot. One of the boys, Dan Monnet, stated that he watched who he thought was Amy in front of the ice cream shop. Also outside and not far away was barber shop owner Jim Kapucinski surveying the parking lot. The cop stopped in front of the boys and even got out of his patrol car to talk with them about skipping class.

Julius Holinek, another classmate, was there also and stated he too saw Amy at the same time and place as the other witnesses. Then at approximately 2:45 p.m., a neatly dressed man in a lightweight beige jacket allegedly walked up to Amy and whispered something in her ear, and they both walked away. A short time later is when she made the telephone call to her mother at work. From that moment on until the body of Amy Renee Mihaljevic was found in February 1990, everyone had held onto their faith that she was still alive and returning soon.

Evidence found at the scene in rural Ashland County, Ohio, suggested that her body had not been in the field for very long. What few facts are known from the guarded coroner's report is that she had been dead for months. Decomposing had been slowed down by her body being kept in a cool place before being dumped. Her last meal had been made up of soy, like what you would find in Chinese takeout or possibly health food products. Amy had eaten spaghetti at school that Friday, so she must have been alive for a few days at least. Cause of death was profuse and continuous bleeding from stab wounds to her neck and throat area.

To date there has been evidence that she was naked when murdered but had not been sexually assaulted. Other reports have noted that her underwear was inside out. Multiple fibers were found and tested against other samples taken from some of the suspects, but nothing has ever been released. Rumors to the furthest limits of imaginations have even circulated around that she had been part of a porn ring of exploited kids. With the hopeful truth to the coroner's report stating Amy was not raped, that falsehood can be put to rest.

Three of the prime suspects openly investigated by the FBI and local authorities were Billy Strunak, Harold Bound, and Raymond Brahler.

Billy Strunak was and is probably one of the most suspected of Amy's death by Bay Village residents. If you believe in profiling, he would fit most of the line items up to and including guilt by his own admission when he committed  suicide thirteen days after her body was discovered. Looking deeper into this man's history though, it is possible he had just come to a point in his life where so much had happened he felt there was no way out. Leaving behind a suicide note saying he was tired of not being able to find a good job, stress, and life itself was not a confession that most people had hoped for.

Two composites, pictured above, were released from witness accounts of a man "5'8 to 5'10, medium build, dark hair. Possibly curly with a bald spot on the top to rear of his head and wearing round glasses and a tan jacket."

There are similarities between Billy Strunak and the first composite drawing. He was known for wearing khaki-type pants and polo pullover shirts with his hair even combed over the same way. He stood five foot seven to five foot eight and had a slender build and light-colored hair. However, considering the second composite and witness accounts of a suspect having possibly curly hair, a bald spot, and wearing glasses, it is not as likely that Strunak was the person seen at the plaza walking with Amy.

Billy was actually an active daily volunteer during the initial search and investigation and helped out in any way he could. With all of the people involved and the police in the same building with Billy, one would think someone would have remembered seeing him at the plaza. When his name did finally surface as a suspect, people began to question his help as a volunteer. Maybe he was just there to track the progress of closing in on the killer?

Some said he was just a weird young man who would sit and stare at women for long periods of time while volunteering at the command post. On at least one occasion, he had sent notes and gifts to Amy's mother, perhaps trying in his own way to possibly offer his condolences? It was discovered partway into the search that Billy had even donated the majority of paper used to print the flyers with Amy's picture. Fellow volunteers felt that was a great gesture until they learned he had stolen it all from his work.

This wouldn't be the first time Billy had stolen from an employer. When police searched his home years earlier on an unrelated incident, they found stolen baseball tickets from the Cleveland Indians, which had been missing from a shipment on a Trailways Bus, where Billy was employed. Police also found women's underwear, lubricant, and condoms along with other stolen items, too many to list.

Local police and FBI questioned him and his siblings on several occasions but never made an arrest. Before things could get any worse for the young man, he mixed up a poisoned concoction drink and took his own life. According to family members, he never knew Amy before the abduction and only knew Margaret Mihaljevic from operating his flea market booth on the weekends, alleging that was why he was so intent on helping find her daughter.

Others painted another picture of this young man. His brother said Billy was always trying to help people. It was just the odd way he went about it that scared everyone. Was Strunak the killer or just a misunderstood man trying to help?

Billy Strunak was never charged, arrested, or tried for the kidnapping and murder of Amy.

Harold Bound, pictured to the left, had served his country in the air force as an intelligence officer for nine years. He had seen a lot of combat back then and was diagnosed as paranoid schizophrenic because of it. But not before receiving the Bronze Star and two Presidential Citations. His connection to the murder was that he lived upstairs over the same riding stables at which Amy spent countless hours in riding lessons during the last summer of her life. Both mother and daughter were seen at Holly Hills Farms a few times a week.

Like Billy Strunak, he was someone people didn't know how to take. His medical condition alone would cause him to appear different, strange, and spooky. It's human nature to admonish or cast blame toward things we can't understand or that scare us. Police focused in on Holly Hills and searched it and the surrounding areas with helicopters and planes using heat-seeking instruments. Lines of FBI agents combed the grounds. Nothing incriminating at the horse stables in connection with Amy's disappearance was ever made public knowledge.

Being a paranoid schizophrenic, Harold felt it was inevitable that he would be arrested for Amy's murder. After the first interview by the FBI, he packed his belongings and tried to be committed to a secured section at a veterans' hospital where he felt the feds could not come after him. A psychiatrist at the center refused to admit him to that facility, so Bound had to settle for a less-restrictive VA center without the military protocols. Government agents were already on his heels and quickly caught up for more intense questioning. The police possibly saw this as a guilty man trying to run.

The FBI felt Harold was a strong enough suspect that they allegedly had him take several polygraph tests and even sodium pentothal, which is a known truth serum. The outcome of those exams was never released and this suspect never arrested. Comparing his features to both composites, Harold Bound wears glasses and his balding is a frontal receding hairline, not top or rear. When reporters asked him point blank if he killed Amy, his response was that he did not.

Harold Bound was never charged, arrested, or tried for the kidnapping and murder of Amy.

Raymond Brahler was a suspect and investigated in the slaying of another young girl with an almost ghostly similarity. Not only was he shopping in the Bay Village Plaza on October 27, 1989, the day Amy was abducted, he was also in Oil City, Pennsylvania, exactly three years to the day from Amy's disappearance when eleven-year-old Shauna Howe was abducted and murdered. Shauna's body was found three days following her murder in a fishing hole not far from home. She died from blunt force trauma and multiple lacerations. Another eerie coincidence was that if you drive down Ashland County Road 1181, where Amy's body was discovered, then turn onto Route 224 you will dead end in Oil City.

Search warrants for his vehicles to attempt to find a match for the gold-colored fibers in both deaths were never carried out by authorities. One saving factor for Ray may have been an accident that almost killed him in 1982 while visiting Oil City. A fall from a faulty wheel on a cable car crippled his right arm so badly that he could barely use it. At one point, he'd hired an attorney because of all the questions and investigations into his life.

Shauna's case remained unsolved until August 2004 when three Oil City men were arrested from DNA samples. Until then, Ray Brahler was the suspect of both murders. Brothers Timothy and James O'Brien of Oil City were convicted of the murder of eleven-year-old Shauna and sentenced to life in prison. A third suspect, Edward Walker, pled guilty but later asked the court to allow him to withdraw his plea and go to trial.

Raymond was never charged, arrested, or tried for the kidnapping and murder of Amy.

Since Amy's abduction, there have been hundreds of leads and multiple suspects. To this date, her murder has not been solved. Has it been a lack of solid evidence to link anyone to her killer, or do the police feel they have yet to positively ID someone?

During the 1980s, there were three other young girls who were abducted and murdered all within this same region of Ohio. Speculation had law enforcement and news media looking at the possibilities of these crimes all being somehow linked together.

Tina Marie Harmon was walking to the grocery store in Creston, Ohio, when she was abducted in October of 1981. She was murdered and her body dumped days later in Navarre, Ohio, in Stark County.

On September 25, 1982, eleven-year-old Krista Harrison of Marshallville, Ohio, was kidnapped, raped, and strangled. Her body was later found in a remote area of Holmes County.

There also was the murder of ten-year-old Deborah Kay Smith, who was enjoying the street carnival in Massillon, Ohio, on June 15, 1983, when someone grabbed her. Deborah's body was found on August 6, 1983, by the Tuscarawas River, near Bolivar, about fifteen miles from her home.

The Wayne County Prosecutor and Sheriff's Department originally charged and convicted two men for the rape and murder of Tina Marie Harmon but later realized they had the wrong men when Robert Buell (pictured to the left), a city planner in Akron, Ohio, became the prime suspect in Krista Harrison's murder.

Prosecutors to this day are still very confident that Buell killed Krista. The fiber and paint evidence was just too strong of a match to doubt his guilt. Investigators had collected several pieces of evidence from the crime scene that matched articles at his residence. Two gloves with orange carpet fibers were found. Also discovered were a clump of hair, a blanket, a green garbage bag with tape on it, and two pieces of a cardboard box with the shipping label sprayed over with black paint that was directly tied to the suspect.

Testing showed that the carpet found at the crime scene matched carpet seized from a van owned by Buell and from Buell's home. Testing also showed that hair samples from Krista and hair samples found at the crime scene were consistent. The court of appeals also agreed that the evidence was overwhelming.

During the trial, which was moved to Cuyahoga County because of publicity, Buell maintained his innocence. He had earlier pled guilty to the abduction and rape of two adult women but always contended he never crossed the line to hurt children. In one interview with the media, he even stated that anyone who would hurt little children should be "fried."

Robert Buell was sentenced to die for Krista's death, and prosecutors felt he killed Tina and Deborah as well but never charged him. Buell argued that the prosecutor knew he was innocent and that there was still a killer on the loose. Just as they carried out his death sentence at the Lucasville State Prison, Buell made his last statement to the parents of Krista Harrison as they administered a lethal dose of chemicals to end his life: "Jerry and Shirley, I didn't kill your daughter. The prosecutor knows that ... and they left the real killer out there on the streets to kill again and again and again. So that some good may come of this, I ask that you continue to pursue this to the end. Don't let the prosecutor continue to spin this out of focus and force them to find out who really killed your daughter. That's all I have to say."

One former law enforcement officer, who asked not to be identified, investigated Buell's contention and came up with some eerie conclusions. This officer was not related to any of the 1980 murder cases of these young girls, and this is his own speculation from investigating Buell's claim of innocence. "If you map out all four girls' abductions and then where their bodies were discovered, you come up with a perfect circle in driving area." Laying out his map of "what if," the officer continued, "All of these murders that occurred in the 1980s were all done

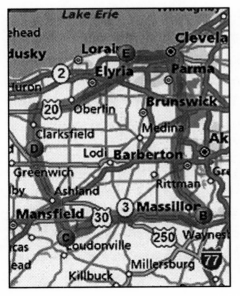

by the same person. Four young girls almost the same age all murdered in less than ten years!"

Is it possible that in the 1980s someone unknown to the police killed all four young girls and is still out there? Hesitating for several seconds, he went on to explain. "Remember, two men had their life sentences overturned when authorities linked Tina Marie Harmon's death to Buell." In Amy and Krista's case, a van was seen. "Gold fibers were supposedly found at the crime scene of Amy's body and orange-colored ones at Krista's. Both are unique colors (or the same) not usually found in vehicles in that time era. Amy was found near New London in Ashland County; Krista was located in northwest Holmes County. Both of those were remote areas near to each other but far away from their homes."

In closing, technically the murders of Tina Maria Harmon and Deborah Kay Smith are "unsolved murders." People want to have closure to these brutal killings, and evidence points to Robert Buell, who killed Krista. Writing this story and offering one person's theory is not meant to reopen those terrible memories, and we offer our sympathy to the families and friends of all murdered victims.

Buell's attorney, Jeffrey Kelleher, in a recent phone conversation summed up his former client and case, "There was nothing simple about Mr. Buell or his case. He was a complex man, and he had a complex case." When asked if he had ever heard his client state who Buell thought committed the murders if he didn't, Kelleher replied that his client had never indicated who he thought committed them. When asked if Buell had a roommate ever living with him during all of this time who may have had access to his vehicle or home, Attorney Kelleher wasn't quite sure but thought a nephew or cousin may have.

The real tragedy is the fact that in less than ten short years, four girls in this region of Ohio all lost their lives at the hands of a cold-blooded and sadistic killer. Neither Krista, Tina, Deborah, nor Amy ever made it to becoming teenagers, never having the opportunity to attend their prom or graduation, get married, and have children of their own. They are gone from their families and they can never come back. Even more tragic than this is the fact that these same types of people who prey on innocent children are still walking the streets in each of our cities and towns every day.

Police still ask for your help with this murder case. They have said not to discount the relevance of any information you may know. Your piece of information may have a significant impact on the investigation when viewed in the context of what they already know.

For further information, contact Bay Village Ohio Police at 440-871-1234, or E-mail Unsolvedmurder07@aol.com, and we will pass along this information.

Research and development of this story was made possible by the Cleveland Public Library, *Plain Dealer* newspaper, Cleveland and Bay Village police, and friends and family of Amy. Special recognition goes to Author James Renner, whose book *Amy: In Search of Her Killer* has brought an in-depth look and renewed interest to law enforcement and everyone connected to her case.

Who Killed Jason Marti?

Wooster, Ohio, is located ideally for anyone wanting to live in a quiet smaller community while also having quick access to larger cities like Canton, Akron, and Cleveland. Having the comfort of being away from the fast pace, high crime rate, and big city traffic congestion attracts more and more people to move to towns like Wooster. Major league football, basketball, huge shopping malls, and other entertainment are all within a short drive.

Home to well-known industry names from Wooster Brush Company to Rubbermaid, this rural area also attracts curious visitors who come to witness the Amish way of life. It is a common sight to view horses and buggies mingling in and out of traffic on any street in the city and throughout all of Wayne County. Everyone appears to be friendly and welcoming to new members of the community and sad when someone moves away.

The closeness is evident in the fact that the city and county law enforcement officers all work from the same judicial complex. Wooster Police and the Wayne County Sheriff's Department are some of the most courteous and visible officers and routinely demonstrate their integrity to protect and serve. It's as though this town has stepped back in time to a place where there is almost the feeling of being able to sleep with your windows open and doors unlocked again. Even Buehler's, the area's largest family-run supermarket chain, has their employees personally load customers' groceries while they sit in the comfort of their own vehicles.

This same Buehler's parking lot area would take up a whole new page in Wooster's history on October 24, 1996, when the body of twenty-one-year-old Jason Marti was discovered by a construction worker as he came to work on a remodeling project at the store. Police theorized that Marti had been lying there since sometime late the night before. Speculation also was that he had died from a close-range handgun blast to the chest. A can of mace and a hammer were found within hand's reach of the body. Shortly after the police arrived and began their investigation, the victim's truck was found parked on the Buehler's lot.

As the day progressed, officers began retracing the activities of the dead man, trying to understand everything that occurred up until the time of death. An autopsy would have to be performed before the exact cause of death was known. Former chief of police Robert Merillat stated repeatedly throughout the day that Jason Marti's death was suspicious but until a coroner's report was produced, he would not say it was definitely a murder. Further information and facts began to surface about the young man's life that suggested a possible motive for foul play.

People make mistakes in their lives, some more than others. Twenty-one-year-old Jason, pictured to the right, had a past that was marked with being in and out of jail for drug-related and firearm charges. One of his crimes allegedly involved a drive-by shooting that sent twenty rounds of bullets into  a West Liberty house and nearby parked car. Even though the gun was never found, police say they were confident he was somehow involved.

Some would conclude right away that if you live by the sword, you die by the sword. According to Jason's girlfriend, family, and friends, he had turned his life around and was no longer involved in any type of criminal activity. His brother Matt and father Dennis both said they could not only tell by "Jay's" words alone that he had abandoned his past life of crime, but it was also evident in his day-to-day life. "He was basically scared straight while he was incarcerated in the Lancaster prison," Dennis said of his son. "Before, if he had been in jail, I could tell he was conning me. This time, he was calling home and the whole tone of his voice had changed."

"I'm not sure what happened while he was in there the last time, but something sure scared the hell out of him." Jason's brother remembers the time he and his brother spent together before the murder. "Before he went to jail the last time, he never really had a lot of time to spend with me or our family. After his release, we often sat for hours just talking and being brothers." Recalling one thing in particular, "Jay came to the house at midnight when I turned sixteen and practically dragged me out the door to go driving saying I was now old enough."

Dennis Marti went deeper into the surrounding events that he feels contributed to his son's killing. "Jay felt so strongly that he had quit his life of misdeeds that he also felt he could change his old 'partners in crime' way of life." Marti went on to say, "I don't think those guys were ready to hear that. It also may have scared them into thinking Jay might turn on them and at some point go to the cops." In fact, according to Jason's dad, his son was allowed to plead to lesser charges and prison time in exchange for his testimony against the actual triggerman in the drive-by shooting he went to prison over.

The elder Marti also says that after his son was killed, none of those other suspects went to trial because "Jay" was to have been the state's star witness. Jason's family freely admits that he was in and out of trouble a lot before his last time being locked up. They say his troubled life began sometime during his senior year at Wooster High School when Jason began skipping class and running with the wrong crowd. Before then, he had a normal childhood with the usual problems most youngsters and teens go through.

Wooster police and court records paint a little bit of a different picture of Jason, saying he was believed to be deeply involved in criminal activity from drug selling, assaults, petty theft, and the drive-by shooting incident for which Jason pled guilty in 1996 to "complicity to improperly discharge a firearm." Jason was a passenger in the drive-by vehicle in what Dennis Marti described as retaliation for an alleged drug deal gone badly. Even the city police may have been somewhat chapped at some of Jason's antics. Family members say he allegedly escaped from the back seat of police cruisers on two occasions after being arrested and handcuffed.

No matter what his lifestyle was before he was released from prison in 1996, his family, friends, and coworkers all agree that Jason had honestly turned his life around and, at least up until his death, was on the straight and narrow path. Whatever mistakes he had made do not make it all right, or legal, to have been murdered in cold blood. And those responsible need to be punished. His father and brother feel 99.9 percent sure his death was at the hands of his former partners in crime. The Martis feel police know their true identities, but no one is cooperating or confessing.

What police do know is that Jason and girlfriend Melissa Burns spent all afternoon together on Wednesday, October 23, 1996. According to Melissa, her boyfriend received a phone call that same evening around 7:00 p.m. from a "friend" asking for help. His last words to her as he left home on North Walnut Street were "I love you, and I'll see you in about an hour." That was the last time she ever saw Jason alive. The coroner's report stated that the fatal bullet entered the left upper chest just below the collarbone, lacerated the aorta, and exited the back of the left chest. It was theorized that Jason was either on his knees or seated on the ground as his killer stood over him.

Police found a set of tire tracks near the body that cut across the lawn to the Northview Alliance Church parking lot. They combed the area with metal detectors, but no bullets or shell casings were found at the site. According to Matt Marti, the can of mace found close to Jason's body must have been his brother's because Jason always carried mace when he had gotten into fights. "Jay wasn't a big guy, so he always tried to mace you first to even the odds." This makes it seem possible that Jason felt something was wrong with the alleged phone call he received so he took the mace and hammer just in case.

Matt and Dennis Marti both agree that because of Jason's alleged deal with the prosecutors to testify against former friends he should not have returned to Wooster after his release from prison. Matt even said, "We kind of expected maybe he would get beat up over this, but not killed!" They also stated that they believed the police had brought in four local suspects for questioning not long after the shooting, but the men "lawyered up," which is the term in this area for hiring a lawyer then refusing to cooperate.

Wooster City Police Chief Steve Thornton confirmed that they had talked to several individuals of interest, but those potential suspects did hire attorneys and refused to speak to law enforcement. He also confirmed that there was video surveillance tape from the Buehler's store, but it did not give them anything solid to work with. "We went as far as to bring in a cold case investigator to go over our reports and findings just to see if we missed anything. We were told everything was done correctly."

Thornton stated that he and members of his department still discuss Jason's death in hopes that with the passing of time someone who may have been afraid or leery to talk at the time of the shooting will now come forward. In closing, the chief went on to say that fears tend to subside after so many years and then the conscience kicks in.

Police still ask for your help with this murder case. They have said not to discount the relevance of any information you may know. Your piece of information may have a significant impact on the investigation when viewed in the context of what they already know.

For further information, call 330-287-5730, or you can E-mail Unsolvedmurder07@aol.com, and we will pass along this information.

Research and development of this story was made possible by the assistance of the *Daily Record*, friends and family of Jason Marti, Wooster City and Wayne County police, and the Wayne County Public Library.

Who Killed Baby Jacob?

Less than four months following Jason Marti's death, another murder occurred in the city of Wooster that shocked everyone beyond belief. Faye Martin came home from work in the early morning hours of March 8, 1997, to find Jacob, her seventeen-month-old son, "blue, cold and lifeless." She ran down to the IGA store near her West Liberty Street apartment to call 911 at 3:08 a.m.

The rescue squad called Wooster police as required for any at-home death while the hospital staff tried unsuccessfully to revive the baby. Jacob Mack's father, Jerry Mack, and his friend Clyde Griffith, pictured below, were the only other people at home all evening with the infant. In fact, police had responded to calls of loud music twice earlier that night but never entered the apartment.

Two weeks after the child's death, the Summit County medical examiner confirmed what police had already suspected. Jacob Mack was murdered on March 8, and the cause of death was "asphyxia due to compression and blunt injuries to the head, chest, trunk, extremities and anus."

Jacob's life had begun two months early as a premature baby on September 16, 1995. Spending those first two months in the hospital due to seizures and other complications, baby Jacob had already  suffered early in life. There are reports of domestic violence with the parents on several occasions. Wooster Police and Social Services had been called to the residence at least once during Jacob's life and noted the baby appeared to be in good health before his murder. Authorities felt all along the death was suspicious and were only waiting on the autopsy reports before openly conducting a murder investigation.

Reports indicated that only the two men were in the residence before, during, and after the infant's death until the baby's mother arrived home at around 2:45 a.m. Clyde Griffith is currently serving the remainder of a ten-year sentence handed down in June of 1997 for aggravated burglary and robbery of an adult female. His sentencing was just three months after Jacob's death. Griffith is in Ohio's Lake Erie Correctional Center. He is due to be released in March of 2009.

Jerry Mack (pictured above), Jacob's father, is living anywhere he can find a place, according to his brother. Currently Jerry Mack is awaiting trial on a petty theft charge in Wayne County Court from a January 2007 arrest. His record dates back years for misdemeanor offenses. Mack's brother says that Jerry drifts from place to place and can't quite get it together. When asked if he thinks Jerry's inability to get his own life straight is related to the death of his son, the older sibling replied, "It's possible."

At the time of the murder, Martin Frantz with the Wayne County Prosecutor's Office said that nothing made him want to prosecute this offense more than after attending Jacob Mack's autopsy. But he has an obligation not to let his emotions pull him away from following the law. And it's very discouraging when he is unable to bring charges against a suspect, even one whom he feels to be guilty without question. Prosecutors and police feel the frustration in this case, but they have a duty to not only the victim but the accused as well.

Sometimes they obtain reliable evidence but have no way of getting it to a jury when no witness will testify. Investigators are hoping even today that someone will come forward and allow Jacob's family closure and justice to the person who committed this unthinkable murder of an infant child. In 2002, Captain Don Edwards said, "I don't think you ever lose the passion to solve a homicide like this one."

Jacob's mother has moved out of the area but remains somewhere in Ohio. Wooster City Police Chief Steve Thornton concurred with most people interviewed that the murder of an infant goes way over the line of decency even in the criminal world. The murder of anyone is unacceptable, but for someone to kill an infant child as brutally as this has to be caught and face justice.

Police still ask for your help with this murder case. They have said not to discount the relevance of any information you may know. Your piece of information may have a significant impact on the investigation when viewed in the context of what they already know.

For further information, call 330-287-5730, or you can E-mail Unsolvedmurder07@aol.com, and we will pass along this information.

Research and development of this story was made possible by the assistance of the *Daily Record*, Wooster City and Wayne County police, and the Wayne County Public Library.

Who Killed Shakira Johnson?

Shakira Johnson, pictured to the right, left her home on September 13, 2003, to attend a block party with the other residents on the east side of Cleveland, Ohio. This was not your old-fashioned type of block party that most people think of. Shakira was  attending a memorial service for slain anti-crime activist Francis Jones on East 106th Street near Benham Road. Shakira, a happy, carefree, beautiful young girl neighbors described as an "angel," never returned home that night to her mother and two brothers on Martin Luther King Boulevard. Her younger brother said he last saw his sister around 4:30 p.m. still on 106th Street with friends.

It's still unclear why the Amber Alert System was not issued by police, but they said her disappearance did not fall under the necessary requirements. Her description though quickly went out to neighbors, local news, and radio as the evening went by. She was described as being four feet seven inches tall and approximately eighty pounds with light-brown eyes and having her sandy-brown hair in a ponytail. On the day she disappeared, Shakira was wearing blue jeans, a white T-shirt, and light-blue tennis shoes.

Everyone in Cleveland, from friends and family to the police and FBI, soon began a massive search for Shakira. Students from her Nathan Hale Junior High also took part in the search. Rallies and other shows of support quickly mounted along with pictures being placed on poles and in windows and handed out in the community. A few days into the search, police and FBI conducted a sweep of the neighborhood, arresting sexual predators wanted on old warrants, hoping their search would turn up the girl or clues.

Cleveland's mayor made a personal visit to Shakira's home to assure her mother they were doing everything possible to bring the little girl home unharmed. Alisa Randle, Shakira's mother, made pleas on TV stations for her daughter's safe return. "Just let her come home please! I just tell everybody to keep her in their prayers. Keep Shakira in your prayers. And whoever has her, just let my baby come home because I know she wants to be home. She needs us, and I need her, and I want her to come home."

Charisse Lyons, twenty-six, of Cleveland, said she had stepped from her house on East Sixty-sixth Street about 8:30 p.m. on September 13, 2003, when she heard a female screaming. She saw a girl who looked like Shakira in the back seat of a red Ford Escort before it left at a high speed. "It was eleven-year-old Shakira Johnson in the back seat screaming at the top of her lungs," Lyons testified. "I didn't know who it was at the time, but I do now." Lyons said the driver wore a hat and had bulging eyes and a rough face.

Police released a description of a vehicle that may have been involved. The car was described as a four-door Ford Escort or Mercury Tracer, clean and bright red in color. It apparently had an older-style license plate and was last seen in the area near East Sixty-first and East Sixty-sixth streets, between Broadway and Union. Lyons later testified in court that she saw the same man in the same red car three times after that. Once he was even pulling out of an East Seventy-first Street field near where Johnson's remains were found. The prosecution says investigators looked into her story, but it didn't pan out.

At the same time, police began to focus specifically on twenty-six-year-old handyman Daniel Hines, pictured to the right, who lived two doors down from one of the places Shakira was last seen. Hines, who was out on bail from an earlier charge that he had allegedly  raped his young female cousin, quickly became the prime suspect. He had been questioned the day of her disappearance and in fact told police he had seen her with friends but he had no personal contact. Hines also stated he had been home all day.

Tyler Fisher, Hines' neighbor, said he and Hines were on their front porches from early afternoon past 11 p.m. on September 13, 2003, the day Shakira vanished from a block party on Hines' East Side street. That account would leave little time for Hines to abduct Shakira from the East 106th Street block party, as prosecutors contend he did.

While he was home, Fisher said, he was on his porch and saw Hines leave his green-over-yellow bungalow only once, for five to ten minutes. "I was outside the whole time," he said. Fisher left his home once to go to the store and was only gone a few minutes. Fisher also made a second trip going to Bedford, Ohio, a short thirty-minute round trip to pick up a friend. As soon as he returned, police stopped by looking for Shakira. Officers spoke briefly to Hines, who stated he had seen Shakira earlier with friends but had no personal contact with the girl. Whether or not Hines was the abductor, the authorities were taking no chances and talked a county judge into revoking the man's bond on September 18, 2003, returning him to jail. With emotions raging and the outcry by the entire city over this crime, it was probably a wise move for Daniel Hines to be back in custody for his own protection. Guilty or not, he was a marked man.

On October 15, 2003, an anonymous tip came in to police stating where they could find the little girl's body. Searching the area described by the caller as a weedy field near East Seventy-first Street, the badly decomposed remains of a small body were discovered just where the caller said they would be. Days later, the coroner announced that it was indeed the body of Shakira Johnson. Funeral services were held days later at the Mount Sinai Baptist Church on Woodland Avenue, and Shakira was buried in Lakeview Cemetery. A very emotional and crowded service was made up of family, friends, city activists, and politicians.

In the meantime, police had already conducted searches of Daniel Hines' home and vehicle, gathering evidence they say linked him to the murder. On November 17, 2003, he was formally charged with one count of aggravated murder and kidnapping. The prosecution stated they were going for the death penalty due to the nature of the killing and her age. Daniel's lawyer, Brett Mancino, contended that his client was innocent and that the real killer was still roaming the streets of Cleveland looking for his next victim, referring to the testimony of Charisse Lyons, who said she saw Shakira being driven away screaming in the back seat of a red car near her home on East Sixty-sixth Street. "This person has never been identified and could be the killer."

By the time Hines' trial for Shakira's murder began, accusations had surfaced that the police had planted a blood-stained glove in Daniel's home that matched the same blood type as the little girl's. There were also claims that the forensic evidence was also tainted because one of the crime scene processors, Joseph Serowik's credibility was in doubt.

Another problem facing the prosecution was their alleged use of a professional jailhouse informant named Videll Schumpert. He claimed Daniel Hines confessed to him how he killed Shakira and that they would never be able to convict him. The defense provided information that showed the informant to be anything but credible.

Then there was the state's own witness who conducted tests relating to bugs found on Shakira's body and a timeline that gave the defense an argument that their client could not have been the killer because he was back in jail at that time. This forensic report questioned the prosecution's case against twenty-six-year-old Daniel Hines. Attorney Mancino argued, "There is no dispute, at least from their side, that the body hadn't been there for more than a few days. If that's true, then Hines could not have dumped the body because he has been in the Cuyahoga Jail since September 18th."

The forensic test is bug science, or entomology. As unpleasant as it may sound, insects and their offspring found on the victim tell scientists many things. In the report, Cuyahoga County's own consultant, Doctor Joe Keiper, suggests Johnson's death could have occurred somewhere between September 23 and October 5. He puts the time of death of Shakira Johnson well after Daniel Hines was in the county jail. The prosecution's theory was that Shakira Johnson was kidnapped, murdered, and her body dumped all on September 13. Her body was concealed until approximately October 11, and then found on the 15. Allegedly, Johnson's body was not in that field for more than a few days before it was discovered.

Defense witnesses testified that Daniel was home all day and only left twice the day Shakira was at the block party, and each time he was only gone for a few minutes and not during the times police say she disappeared.

Prosecutors stand by their belief that Daniel is the killer and that certain crucial evidence was not allowed into the trial. Daniel was acquitted by the jury of the murder of Shakira Johnson. He was also later found innocent of the alleged rape charges against his cousin. According to his lawyer, Brett Mancino, numerous people have made it a point to let him and Daniel know that they always believed he was innocent of killing Shakira. Mancino also states that the true key to solving the murder is the man in the red car and events surrounding the abduction and murder of Shakira as described by Charisse Lyons.

If anything positive came from her death, the police were able to make other arrests of wanted sex offenders in Shakira's neighborhood because of her disappearance and subsequent search. Hopefully those arrests saved another child from being raped, kidnapped, and/or murdered. Since 1997, convicted sex offenders have to register in the communities where they live under Ohio's "Megan's Law." Megan's Law was named after Megan Kanka, a New Jersey girl murdered in 1994 by a twice-convicted sex offender. As a result, there are now three basic classifications for the sex offenders in Ohio.

A **sexually-oriented offender** is someone who has committed a sexually-oriented crime. That person has to register with the county for ten years with no community notification. A **habitual sex offender** is someone who has committed repeated sex crimes. It requires registration for twenty years but still no community notification. A **sexual predator** means the offender must register every ninety days for the rest of his or her life and the community is notified. The difference with this designation is the possibility of future offenses. The prosecutor has to show by clear and convincing evidence that an offender is going to commit a future offense.

Is it reasonable that all neighborhoods should be notified anytime anyone convicted of any child sex crime lives or moves into their neighborhoods? Just ask Shakira's mother that question.

If Daniel Hines was not the killer as the jury believed, then the only other evidence and sighting of Shakira was on September 13, 2003, after 4:30 p.m. by Charisse Lyons, who said she had stepped from her house on East Sixty-sixth Street at about 8:30 p.m. when she heard a girl screaming. She saw someone who looked like Shakira in the back seat of a red Ford Escort before it left at a high speed. It apparently had an older-style license plate and was last seen in the area near East Sixty-first and East Sixty-sixth streets, between Broadway and Union. Lyons later testified in court she saw the same man in the same red car three times after that. Once she claims he was even pulling out of an East Seventy-first Street field near where Johnson's remains were found.

Most assuredly, the person who owned this car has either traded or sold it by now. But, this vehicle is probably still being driven in the Cleveland area by a new owner, and that person may have even purchased it from the murderer himself.

In November 2005, Daniel Hines filed a federal civil rights suit against the City of Cleveland and named the prosecutor's office and investigators for violating his rights during the investigation, which led to his arrest and later being found not guilty by a jury. In a media interview, County Prosecutor Bill Mason said about the lawsuit, "He ought to be thanking his lucky stars that he is not spending this Thanksgiving in prison rather than making scurrilous accusations against the police."

Also in 2005, on the two-year anniversary of his sister's disappearance, fifteen-year-old LaQuan Johnson pleaded for her killer to turn himself in. "Come forward and take responsibility for what you've done," he said, standing tall with an arm around his mother. "Bring justice to my sister and peace to my family."

The thought that Shakira Johnson's killer is still out there haunts those who gathered Tuesday night on the corner of East 110th Street and Union Avenue in Cleveland, near where the eleven-year-old girl was last seen. The vigil drew about forty people to mark the second anniversary of the day Shakira vanished from a block party near her East Side home.

Police still ask for your help with this murder case. They have said not to discount the relevance of any information you may know. Your piece of information may have a significant impact on the investigation when viewed in the context of what they already know.

For further information, call 216-621-1234, or you can E-mail Unsolvedmurder07@aol.com, and we will pass along this information.

Research and development of this story was made possible by the *Plain Dealer* newspaper, Cleveland Police, friends and family of Shakira Johnson, and Daniel Hines' attorney, Brett Mancino.

Who Killed Mary Leonard & Kevin Beard?

Jerry Leonard was sitting on a neighbor's Thayer Street front porch relaxing on August 24, 1979, when he noticed his sister getting out of a car two houses up. Mary had just returned home from her job at Acme supermarket in Cuyahoga Falls. The younger brother noticed she was carrying a bag of Doritos corn chips as she walked over to where he was. He grabbed the bag from her hands, but she quickly snatched it back before he could take any of the chips.

Mary went home and up the stairs to get ready for her date with Ricky Beard, her longtime boyfriend. Mary Leonard was a good daughter in every sense of the word. Growing up, her parents were proud of the way their daughter was maturing into a young woman. She had just finished her junior year at North High with honors and merits. Taking the job at Acme markets was giving her some responsibility and the opportunity to earn some money. Ricky was from the same mold of teenager. At nineteen, he had graduated from the same high school and was working for the William Ley Company as a laborer. Both showed signs of taking on responsibility and earned the respect of their families.

This night they were headed to an evening showing of the *Amityville Horror* movie at the Ascot Drive In Theatre on Akron-Cleveland Road in Northampton Township. Ricky Beard showed up a short time after Mary arrived home driving his 1972 blue and white Chevy Impala, which he took great care of and pride in. His car was his second love; Mary Margaret Leonard was his first.

Both teens, pictured below, were last seen around midnight on the Leonards' front porch swing by a neighbor who remembers waving to the kids and seeing Ricky's car parked in front.

 Sometime between then and daylight, something that began as a mysterious disappearance of two young teenagers turned into something much worse. No one realized the kids were missing until around 7 a.m., when the phone rang at the Leonard home. It was Mr. Beard looking for his son as he had not yet returned home. A quick check of Mary's room showed her bed empty and un-slept in from the night before. Both teens had always kept their curfews, so the parents knew something wasn't right.

Not too far away on Northampton Road and Portage Trail, Patrolman Ronald Kolenz spotted Ricky's car abandoned on a farm road with a possible bullet hole in the passenger-side windshield. Looking inside, the officer noticed there were no keys but Beard's wallet was on the floorboard. There was no evident sign of blood or any foul play except for the hole in the windshield, which could have already been there.

Over the course of the next six years, there was a lengthy investigation and search, which started with days of the police, volunteers, and bloodhounds on the ground while the Air National Guard helicopter was searching by air. Psychics Laurie Campbell and Pam Coronado were later brought in, and the Leonard family even hired famed Private Investigator William Dear, who held national claim to solving these types of cases. No one could locate any trace of the teens or assist the police with solid clues or suspects. In all, it was one of the most intense missing persons cases ever conducted by the Akron Police Department.

Then on May 29, 1985, someone not related to the case made a grisly discovery while operating a backhoe only two miles from where Ricky Beard's abandoned car was found. Skeletal remains were discovered. Jerry Leonard recalled in an interview with the Akron newspaper the day his manager at work got a call to send him home. "When I got home, everybody was there. Some remains were found." They were waiting for the coroner to show up at the house. When he arrived, he stated that it was "definitely Mary." "Everybody started crying"; then someone asked, "What about Ricky?" And the coroner said, "Yes." They'd found Mary's pocketbook and ID and even the knife Ricky always carried with him wherever he went.

Jerry and some others drove out to the site to see what they could discover of the finding. "I saw sheets with bones lying there. I saw Mary's skull. Her watch was still on her wrist. One of the guys showed me a shoulder blade with a hole in it. It was Ricky's." Early findings showed a knife injury in the rib area of Mary's body. County Coroner Dr. William Cox said that the bullet hole in Beard "went from the back of his body to the front of his body." He also stated, "We consider the manner of deaths as homicides."

Their skeletal remains were then shipped to the Smithsonian Institution in Washington DC for further examination by a physical anthropologist. The final report indicated that there was evidence that their wounds were "overkill." Ricky and Mary both had received multiple gunshot wounds, and Mary had been stabbed at least once in the chest as well. Doctor Cox stated, "When you see that kind of overkill, you think of a motorcycle gang killing. They will shoot and stab a person multiple times."

In 1985, police said they had few clues or theories to go on. One alleged possibility was that Ricky had somehow been involved in drugs. In the ashtray of his Impala, police found approximately seventeen marijuana cigarette butts and some methamphetamine pills. Could their deaths have been from events surrounding drugs, or were they somehow in the wrong place at the wrong time? Ricky's mother swore that her son had no dealings in drugs, and Mary's family knew their daughter too well to believe that.

By the year 2000, investigators had all but shelved their case as being unsolved when new suspects and "persons of interest" began to surface. Detectives quickly reacted and reopened the case. As far as they were concerned, there was no such thing as a closed murder investigation. They had only been waiting patiently for new information, and now it appeared to be coming their way. Sgt. Edward Moriarty was a longtime Akron police officer, and along with brother and sister officers Ed and Janet Mathews, they spent countless hours searching out leads and leaving no piece of information not followed up on.

Few factual leads have left the Leonards not holding out much hope that they will one day have closure with an arrest. Their biggest disappointment came when they hired famed Private Investigator William Dear out of Texas to come to Ohio and assist in the case. Ron Leonard said the family had spent a lot of money with "no results" and had not received specific information about his findings. Dear stated that he sent numerous reports and findings to the family and police.

To date, police have not been able to make any arrests in the case, but they are still hopeful that someone will come forward and provide the information needed to solve this murder mystery that has lasted twenty-seven years. Detective Moriarty has been with the Akron Police Department since the time of Mary and Ricky's disappearance, so he has both the professional and personal drive to see justice for the two teens and to try to bring some type of closure to the Beard and Leonard families. "We have been narrowing it down to a list of viable suspects." Police are hopeful that announcing the re-opening of the case will bring people forward who had been reluctant to talk years ago out of fear. "Hopefully, something will come in to us. Everyone remembers this case," says Moriarty.

The Leonard family, pictured on the next page, is very happy that police are looking into the case again and would like to count on people to now come forward. Mary's younger brother says someday he would like to be able to tell his kids why their aunt is gone. "It would be nice to know why she was taken from us." Gloria Leonard, Mary's mother, says she misses her the most during the holiday season.

Luanne Eddy says she thinks about her brother Ricky whenever it snows. He always plowed the driveway with the family truck. Whether or not their killers are ever caught, both families know in their hearts that regardless of whatever happened to Mary and Ricky so long ago there won't be a day that goes by that they won't be thought of and missed.

Police still ask for your help with this murder case. They have said not to discount the relevance of any information you may know. Your piece of information may have a significant impact on the investigation when viewed in the context of what they already know.

For further information, contact the Akron Police Department at 330-375-2490, or you can E-mail Unsolvedmurder07@aol.com, and we will pass along this information.

Research and development of this story was made possible by the assistance of the *Akron Beacon Journal*, friends and family of Mary Leonard and Ricky Beard, Akron City Police, and the Summit County Public Library's Reference Department.

Who Killed Four Summit County Women in 18 Weeks?

Janice Christensen, JoAnn Bartholomew, Marcia Kay Piotter, and Barbara Blatnik never knew each other in life even though all lived nearby in upper-middle-class homes. They also had other common threads that forever hold them together as a group. Each was viciously murdered within a small geographical area and in a time period of slightly over four months combined. Another connection these women share is that their killer(s) remain unknown.

Janice Christensen, thirty-one, went out to jog before meeting her mother for lunch on August 10, 1987. Being somewhat of an exercise enthusiast, she enjoyed the times she was able to run, and this morning she would take on the Metro Parks Bike and Hike Trail, which was always a challenge for endurance. As she left her and husband Ken's residence on Quick Road in Cuyahoga Falls, this would be the last time Janice would ever be home. The initial concerns would come soon after when she did not show up for lunch with her mother. When Ken found that she was not back by the time he arrived, they knew something was terribly wrong. Had she been hurt while running and fell, knocking herself unconscious? Or had his wife gone over to a friend's home and just forgot to let him know? Making phone calls long into the night, Ken was unable to locate his wife. Friends and relatives came by, and they planned to search for her together at daybreak.

Waking early the next morning, her husband quickly took to the trail with their dog Wolf. It would be their seventy-pound pet who would locate Janice by the scent of her body. Ken darted into the brush where the dog had stopped and began noticeably acting odd. Not knowing at first if she were alive or dead, he felt her cold body and then noticed the dried blood on her shirt. After running to the nearest home he could find, Ken called the police. The coroner later stated that she had died at about 10 a.m. the day before. She had been sexually assaulted and then stabbed to death.

Police had no clues, suspects, or any evidence to tie this murder to any others over the previous few years. What they had yet to learn was that there would be three more murders almost identical to each other in just a matter of weeks.

It was bitterly cold the night of October 21, 1987, when forty-six-year-old JoAnn Bartholomew of Stow left evening church service at the First Church of God in Tallmadge, which was the same house of worship she had been baptized and married in. Church was a very big part of her life, so was communication between husband and wife in letting each other always know where the other was going to be and when each would be home. Chuck Bartholomew did not attend the services that night because they were in the process of building a new Dairy Queen in Medina to go with their first store in Cuyahoga Falls. He wanted to finish some of the drywalling in the office. JoAnn left the church and stopped by the Chapel Hill Mall to get some things early for Christmas.

Mr. Bartholomew returned home at approximately 9:30 p.m. and found his wife was not home. This wasn't alarming because she sometimes went to after-service meetings at the church. But sometime around midnight, when his young son woke him on the couch looking for his mother, Chuck hurriedly searched the house and garage for any signs of her. Taking the route his wife would have taken to church, he drove in search of JoAnn's car. Never considering the mall lot, he soon returned home, hoping she would be there.

Sunrise the same morning found Chuck Bartholomew and son in his car once again driving and searching. Finally turning into the mall, he spotted her Cadillac. After notifying the police, they asked him to check inside the trunk to make sure her body wasn't in there. It wasn't. Several days later, after a frantic family search of the area, her partially nude body was discovered behind the Best Product store at the mall. She had been raped and stabbed to death just like Janice Christensen.

A reward fund was started for any information leading to the arrest and conviction of her killer. Donations totaled $3,000. Now a panic was brewing amongst the area's citizens. Was there a mysterious serial killer on the loose? The police had no leads or information to pin down suspects on either murder. People's day-to-day outings now seemed to be more controlled. Looking over your shoulder and making sure car doors were immediately locked after getting in were just some precautions taken. Gun sales were up and crisis hotline phones were ringing continuously with callers asking what all could be done for their safety.

Days later, some of Mrs. Bartholomew's personal belongings began to surface in different areas of the city. Some credit cards and her purse were found near Patterson Park, and other items were discovered near North Main Street and East Cuyahoga Falls Avenue.

It was now Monday, December 14, 1987. Akron resident Marcia Kay Piotter, thirty-six, was making sure that she openly cautioned her family and friends to be careful when outside because of the recent killings of Christensen and Bartholomew. Taking those same precautions herself anywhere she went wasn't good enough to keep her from becoming victim number three. Even though there was the fear of a killer on the loose, it did not stop Marcia or her parents from attending bingo at St. Martha's Catholic Church located at 300 East Tallmadge Avenue. Fred and Joan Fisher, her parents, walked her out afterwards to ensure she safely made it to her car. Marcia hadn't won any money, but she loved to play the game nonetheless.

The next morning, her husband, Larry, called everyone he could think of looking for his wife, including the police. It definitely was not like his wife not to come home. Marcia's parents and others searched in the snowy conditions for her but to no avail. Sometime around 1 a.m. the phone rang, and it was the police asking for Mr. Piotter to come to the hospital about his wife. Marcia's four-door 1987 Oldsmobile Cutlass was found in an apartment complex parking lot on North Pershing Avenue. When the police arrived, they found her body slumped over the front seat stabbed to death. She was only six blocks from home. The only difference in this murder was she had not been sexually assaulted.

Pure panic now not only engulfed the area residents but caused the police to also be on high alert. Gun sales were up drastically, and talk of the invisible killer was on the lips and minds of residents. Several law enforcement agencies in Summit County formed a task force to investigate and find similarities in the killings. No leads were  coming in, and it appeared nothing could be done to stop the murderer from striking again.

Saturday, December 19, 1987, was only six days before Christmas. Barbara Blatnik was seventeen years old and probably hadn't given any thought to being a casualty of the killer since the other females were much older than her. Being a teenager, she could only think of the party she was going to be attending that night. A junior at Cleveland's Erieview Catholic High School, she had lots of friends to meet Saturday night, and it was close enough to their home in Garfield Heights that her parents, John and Terri Blatnik, allowed their daughter to go.

According to newspaper interviews, Barbara's mother says she knew the moment her daughter died that night. Terri Blatnik recalls seeing her daughter in a dream going through a tunnel of bright light. In her dream, Terri said, her daughter told her, "I love you, Ma, but I have to go." When she told her husband, he just dismissed it until they got the news later about their daughter. At 3 p.m. Sunday afternoon, two police officers showed up at the Blatniks' home, asking John to accompany them to Akron to identify what they believed to be his daughter's body.

Police told the father that the girl they had found had been strangled and raped, and that she was wearing a school ring with "Barbara" inscribed inside. Investigators felt that since she had been strangled and not stabbed, this was a different murderer than the other three. Evidence also proved that she was raped by more than one person. Barbara was able to leave the police a clue as to who her killer may have been by a message scrawled in the palm of her hand shortly before she died.

Police had stated that the message appeared to be numbers and words. Her hand was amputated and sent to Washington DC for analysis. It is not known what the results of those tests concluded. Some have speculated she may have written them while at the party, not at the time of her death. The task force investigating the rash of murders also felt that her murder was not related to the three older women who were stabbed and only sexually assaulted by one person.

Radio station WNIR began a call-in program to discuss on air citizens' fears and speculation as to who committed these crimes. Radio disc jockeys actually stated that they had all but solved the murders even though police had no solid evidence or suspects themselves. Law enforcement was quick to state that the radio show was interfering with their investigation and that the talk show hosts were just jockeying for ratings and controversy. Some callers even claimed the killer was a man dressed as a nun, woman, or as a doctor.

Police felt a break come their way on January 23, 1988, when an abduction attempt was foiled by a woman who fought off her knife-wielding attacker as he tried to drag her between two cars at 12:30 a.m. The victim was walking to her home when the assault occurred. She struck the attacker in the groin, and he dropped his knife and ran. She described him as a white male with a mustache, about five feet ten inches tall and weighing approximately 165 pounds. The knife was turned over to the Summit County coroner for tests to see if there was a connection to the other recent murders. Later reports indicated they were not related.

Despite a massive investigation, neighborhood watches, and vigilance in the citizens taking extreme precautions, four women were murdered in just eighteen weeks in close proximity. And to date, none have been solved. In fact, with the similarities and short time frames in which they all occurred, police can't say for sure if it was the work of a serial killer or not. What they do agree on is that these murders are very haunting insomuch as no one was ever arrested and/or convicted. They pursued every lead and utilized their best efforts but came up with nothing.

In 1997, ten years after his wife's murder, Ken Christensen told the *Akron Beacon Journal* that he is "scared of not seeing the killer's face." He goes on to say, "The thing is, I don't want to die first before I see him. I can't say what I would like to do to the guy. I'd like to see him dead." Christensen said that he could no longer stay in the same town that he and his wife lived in. He and his wife had made plans to move to Florida before her death, so he decided to move there and start over.

Chuck Bartholomew was looking for answers to what happened the night his wife was murdered. He was able to release his anger and frustrations by running at night where he could be out by himself and let out his grief and hostilities toward the killer. He remarried years later but still has the need to find JoAnn's killer. Talking to the news media in 2000, Chuck said, "When people commit crimes, they have to tell somebody. I can't believe that the person who committed this crime is the only person who knows it. I think there are others who know."

Bartholomew said in closing, "And if the person or persons are found, I have to know what happened that night. I need to know every detail. And I want to know why."

Joan and Fred Fisher, parents of Marcia Piotter, joined several support groups to help with the loss of their daughter. Mrs. Fisher stated that her husband never got over the loss. "It affected him a lot. I can't say fathers love a daughter more than mothers do, but daughters are special to a father."

Terri Blatnik, mother of Barbara, said she very much wants the case solved but did not think she could ever meet her daughter's killer face to face. "I'm terrified of going into closure; I'm so scared of going ten years back that I don't know if I can survive it again." But she says, "I don't hate this person because he is going to pay." She hopes that he sees her daughter every time he closes his eyes.

Almost four years later, another strange chain of events had Akron investigators at first weighing the possibilities that the same killer may have resurfaced with a slightly different style for murdering his victims. Police say it is not uncommon for killers to change their MO and become more vicious.

Twenty-three-year-old Rachael M. Johnson of Tallmadge Road was last seen on March 30, 1991, with her best friend after leaving the El Cid bar on East Tallmadge Avenue. According to the unidentified female, she and Rachael left the bar around 2:30 a.m. and drove towards Johnson's home. A tire on the girlfriend's car went flat near Fouse and Glenwood, so instead of waiting, Rachael decided to walk home because she was paying a babysitter to watch her daughter.

Except for her killer, this would be the last time anyone saw Rachael Johnson alive. Her body was found in northeast Akron stabbed ten times, raped, beaten, and thrown into the street still possibly alive. Then she was doused with a flammable liquid and set on fire. Police say she was abducted by someone who may have actually damaged the tire so it would go flat. Johnson was unidentified until her friend saw the story in the paper and prayed it was not Rachael.

A loving single mother of a three-year-old little girl, Ms. Johnson had been going through hard times but kept her spirits high and was devoted to her daughter, Katelyn. The last thing friends remember Rachael talking about was being excited to color Easter eggs with her daughter.

Police were investigating any possible ties to the deaths of Janice, JoAnn, and Marcia. The only prime suspect ever named by police in her murder was then twenty-one-year-old Daniel Wilson, who has been convicted of murdering at least one other woman by setting her on fire. But DNA samples were inconclusive, and he was never charged, arrested, or convicted of Rachael's murder. Wilson had been convicted at the age of fourteen for killing an eighty-one-year-old man and served time in a juvenile detention center.

Police still ask for your help with this murder case. They have said not to discount the relevance of any information you may know. Your piece of information may have a significant impact on the investigation when viewed in the context of what they already know.

For further information, call 330-375-2490, or you can E-mail Unsolvedmurder07@aol.com, and we will pass along this information.

Research and development of this story was made possible by the assistance of the Reference Department of the Akron-Summit County Public Library, friends and family of the victims, and the Akron City Police records.

Who Killed Pamela Terrill?

In the 1970s, Medina County, Ohio, would be marred by alleged county corruption and hatred between political families that included Democratic and Republican feuding judges, county commissioners, and a prosecutor. The older generation of Medina's residents remember all too well the years of bickering and family squabbles that ultimately governed their lives. Unlike the famous Hatfield and McCoy feud, these members of the Whitfield and Happs clans held political and legal power they allegedly were not afraid to use for their own personal gains.

On August 12, 1976, twenty-one-year-old Pamela Terrill was allegedly attacked sexually by her boss at the Horizon Prince T-shirt Company in Medina. Her accused assailant was Mark Whitfield, who had just previously won the Republican election for county commissioner in 1976. His father was retired Medina Common Pleas Judge Neil Whitfield. Pamela reportedly told her friends that she was "afraid for her life" after reporting her boss to the authorities.

What happened eleven days later would send the county into a spiral descent that would last for at least the next twelve years and is still on the minds and lips of people today. A story of sex, corruption, murder, and cover-ups that would make as excellent a made-for-TV show today as the one Pamela Terrill was actually watching on television the night she mysteriously died in 1976.

Pamela was watching the TV movie *Winter Kill* on August 22, 1976, with her boyfriend in Beresa. They watched the intense movie about a string of unsolved murders that haunted a small town in New England. She left around 11 p.m. and reportedly went home to her apartment on East Liberty Street that she shared with her twenty-two-year-old sister, Cynthia. The older Terrill was dating attorney Gregory Happ, and they returned to the apartment around 2:30 a.m. It appeared that Pamela was asleep in her bedroom. Happ reported leaving at 3:30 a.m., and everything appeared to be fine.

At approximately 7:30 a.m. that same morning, Cynthia was awakened by a phone call from Horizon Prince asking why Pamela was not at work. Figuring her sister overslept, Cynthia went to her room and upon going into the walk-in closet found Pamela's body on the floor. It appeared she had been strangled. Her mouth had been covered by cellophane tape, and there were bruises on her neck. The coroner initially concluded that Pamela hung herself by standing in a wicker basket and looping a green scarf over the hook in the closet. "Strangulation with a smooth object." Contrary to that statement was another report that her neck bore a "deep reddish grey groove from a wire, rope or clothesline."

Before the Terrill family could demand an autopsy, her body had been embalmed and the tape on her mouth, which probably had evidence of fingerprints, had disappeared. The murder scene at the apartment was never sealed off, and as many as twenty people had gained access to the residence. The alleged scarf and other items were never sent to a forensic lab, and somehow the scarf was even destroyed accidentally by police. Cynthia told police that even though there were no signs her sister had a visitor that night, a back door that was kept locked was not locked.

There were accusations that the police intentionally failed to take several steps to secure the area and evidence. At least one police officer stated that the case was intentionally slowed by superiors. Pamela's family fought to have the coroner's ruling of suicide overturned. Based on the following facts and events, the coroner later ruled her death "undetermined." The closet hooks were tested and only found to support approximately fifty pounds of weight before coming out of the wall. A psychological evaluation was conducted by David Greth, and after reviewing her lifestyle and emotions at the time of her death, it appeared to him suicide was "highly unlikely." She appeared to be happy and enjoying life. Also there was no suicide note. And when her body was found, she was nude, and most female suicide victims don't want to be found that way.

Cynthia signed an affidavit that stated her sister's body was not hanging when she discovered it. There also was the rumor and idea that Pamela had died from strangulation due to a sexual asphyxiation practice that is said to increase pleasure. Some people close to the investigation believed that Pamela was murdered by her former boss, County Commissioner Mark Whitfield. James Butler with the prosecutor's office stated in writing that "the primary suspect, if the death was a homicide, would be Mark Whitfield."

At that time, Whitfield said he had an alibi of being at a party with numerous other people including his wife. Police admit they never interviewed guests to verify his being there. He later changed his story to say he was either at his father's home or his own at the approximate 12:30 a.m. time of her death. More conflicts in the case became evident when two separate coroners gave different beliefs of what caused her death. Then there was the question of Terrill's actual autopsy being performed by Doctor Volodkevich, a friend of then county judge Neil Whitfield, who had presided over the doctor's recent divorce.

As the investigation was starting to come to a dead end and police were about to close the case, Mark Whitfield's darker lifestyle began to emerge—a family secret that Mark was a cross dresser who loved to dress up as a woman. On April 5, 1979, Whitfield was stopped by the sheriff's department for allegedly trying to break into a woman's house in Liverpool Township. What they discovered was the county commissioner of two years was dressed as a woman and wearing a blond wig. Whitfield assured the deputies he would seek professional counseling if they would keep his secret. And the victim's family decided not to press charges.

Whether or not Mark Whitfield ever sought professional help is not known for sure. Years later he would be implicated as the alleged person who made headlines in the *Akron Beacon Journal* and *Plain Dealer* in Cleveland when dress designer Diane Marshall notified police that a strange incident of a man fitting Whitfield's description hired her to create a dress for him. He had made several appointments before finally showing up using a phony name and phone number.

Their alleged meeting to create the dress was startling to the designer when the man came out of the dressing room wearing a stuffed bra and pantyhose he had brought with him. But what gave her the cold chills and caused the concern that led her to police was the fact that the man requested as a favor to "call me Pam." Whoever the man was that ordered the dress never returned to pay or pick up his designer gown.

Whitfield being stopped by the sheriff's department dressed as a woman and some new information into Pamela's alleged murder opened new directions for the investigation. Three months later, Mark Whitfield resigned as Republican county commissioner. All along it was widely felt that Gregory Happ was behind part of the drive to solve Terrill's murder because of his connection with their family. In fact, it was Happ who had disproved facts surrounding her death in both the coroner and police findings.

His displeasure in the county's governing body is what caused him to seek public office. He openly criticized Judge Whitfield and his son Mark even while Happ was prosecuting attorney for four years in Medina County. He never denied his feelings and outspoken views about the Whitfield family, and stated, "It's no big secret." It's also believed that Happ was behind the two petitions to oust the judge from office and may have actually been part of the driving force that caused Whitfield to retire early from the bench.

Responding to residents' comments that he may have been behind the reopening of Pamela Terrill's investigation and that it was politically motivated, he responded by saying, "People want to put it off as politics. The investigation of Pam Terrill is not political. It's a tragic event of a girl whose murder has never been solved."

Was there a bungling and cover-up of Pamela's murder? Enough people felt so that a special grand jury was set up to investigate not only her mysterious death but several others that reeked of a possible cover-up to conceal corruption in Medina County. In 1980, Charles A. Witenhafer, a Liverpool Township cement contractor and bookmaker, was found bludgeoned to death in the basement of his home. That case was turned over to four Summit County deputies to investigate. Two Medina lawyers were impaneled as prosecutors, but no charges were ever filed.

The other suspicious unsolved murder was that of Harry L. Sugden, a forty-eight-year-old International Salt company employee from Michigan who was found dead in a motel on January 30, 1977. His death was ruled a suicide even though County Coroner Andrew Karson did not perform an autopsy or other tests to come to that conclusion.

Other allegations being looked into were the Medina City Police's handling of seized property, office records, and weapons disposal. Civil Service records from 1969 to check for improprieties surrounding Homer Davis succeeding his father as the Medina chief of police raised the question of whether Homer had been placed as chief without considering other more qualified prospects. Davis beat out five other qualified applicants to assume the job. Also, there were logs and records from calls answered by the police in regards to claims that Davis interfered with investigations up to and including Pamela's death.

Judge Whitfield was to be investigated for allegedly using his political position to aid his son Mark in obtaining a $120,000 loan from a bank for his failing T-shirt business. Then three months later, his son filed bankruptcy. Whitfield then reportedly sold his defunct T-shirt company to famed pro-football player Franco Harris before the bankruptcy was discharged by the court. Grand jury inquiries were said to be looking at the possible surroundings of the death of Marjorie Whitfield, wife of the judge and Mark's own mother.

According to reports, Mrs. Whitfield's death was ruled a suicide from an alleged overdose of insulin in 1981, even though news media accounts stated that she was not a diabetic. A Medina investigator allegedly stated that he was assigned to look into her death but was taken off the case by then chief of police Homer Davis when he asked to interview the judge and Mark Whitfield regarding the events surrounding her death.

In 1986, Medina officials requested that the FBI and U.S. Attorney's Office conduct an investigation into the corruption going on in the county. U.S. Attorney Patrick McLaughlin responded by saying his office didn't have jurisdiction because no federal crimes had been committed. Finally in September of 1987, the grand jury was impaneled and led by Special Prosecutor Peter Hull. The order was signed by retired Cuyahoga County judge Robert Feighan. In his order, Feighan wrote that public interest requires a special grand jury to examine allegations of corruption and favoritism in Medina County government.

A panel of twelve people would now sit and listen carefully to scores of witnesses, from police officers to former politicians and government employees. Supposedly the main focus was to be on the suspicious death of Pamela Terrill, but Special Prosecutor Hull made no qualms that his investigation would cover every aspect of the alleged corruption that was believed to have gone on for years.

Pamela's body was exhumed on or around July 16, 1987, for another autopsy to be performed by Cuyahoga County Coroner Elizabeth Balraj and a pathologist, Dr. Robert Challener. Her grave bore only a plastic wreath and worn-out nameplate with Pamela's name on it. The only other identification to find her grave is site #38 in the Columbia Township Cemetery. None of her family was present when her body was exhumed. The autopsy was meant to try to determine if her death was a murder or not.

From the grand jury's work came an indictment against Mark Whitfield, pictured to the left, for the murder of Pamela Terrill. They also indicted him for the rape that they believed occurred on or around August 12, 1976, just a few days before Whitfield was accused of murdering her. Twelve years later, on May 2, 1988, the murder trial began that everyone hoped would put a close to the years of speculation surrounding the twenty-one-year-old girl's death. Whitfield elected not to be tried by a jury, a risky or crafty gamble by the defendant to allow the decision of his fate to rest solely on the integrity and fair reputation of Judge James McMonagle from Cuyahoga County.

In opening statements, the state contended that defendant Mark Whitfield murdered Ms. Terrill to keep her from prosecuting the sexual assault she had reported to police two weeks before her death and that her murder was committed by a transvestite to make it look like an accidental, autoerotic death. Prosecutors painted a picture of Whitfield being a transvestite who had not only raped and murdered Pamela but was a fixated sexual deviant with a bizarre taste for blondes like the deceased. This included testimony from one blonde witness alleging Mark had fondled her on their way to Pamela's funeral.

One Medina detective testified that the police chief tried to stall his efforts to investigate Mark Whitfield as a suspect. Detective James Dunkle stated that evidence at the scene of Pamela's apartment turned up missing. Dunkle also testified that the coroner, Andrew Karson, failed to secure the crime scene area to allow them to collect evidence.

When asked earlier if he felt then chief of police Davis did or said anything to hamper the investigation, the officer said yes.

Wanda Vasil testified that Whitfield stalked her at least twice while he was dressed as a woman. Sheriff's Deputy Warren Walter testified he was the officer who stopped Mark, who was dressed as a woman, as he drove away from the scene of the burglary at Vasil's home in April 1979. Whitfield was reportedly wearing a full-length dress with flowers on it, nylons, and a wig. He was also wearing makeup and lipstick. He admitted to the deputy to being at the lady's house twice before while dressed that way. Whitfield was never charged with any crime even though Mrs. Vasil stated he had continued to stalk her after that.

Also testifying was Diane Marshall, who was contacted then visited by a man who claimed to be Mark Wood wanting her to make a dress for him. Marshall told the court about the incident where she was asked to call the man by his feminine name, which was Pam. While on the stand, she pointed to Mark Whitfield as the man who had been to her shop requesting the gown. Laura Kaspar Mackell had worked with Pamela in 1976 at the T-shirt shop. She testified of one occasion in which Whitfield suddenly showed up at an apartment of a friend she was visiting and began making advances at her. "I pushed him back, and he continued coming towards me" and would not leave until she threatened to tell his wife.

Pamela was said to have been involved in a sexual autoerotic behavior that ultimately led to her death. A sexual partner may or may not be involved in the act; however, if one is excluded, the practice can be referred to as autoerotic asphyxiation, or AEA. Various methods are used to achieve the level of oxygen depletion needed, such as a plastic bag over the head or self-strangulation, typically by the use of a scarf.

The increased pleasure results from the body producing more endorphins as it approaches the state of asphyxia. Pleasurable or not, it is an extremely dangerous practice that results in many accidental deaths each year. Ironically enough, it was Mark Whitfield who first mentioned this type of behavior and possible way she had died to investigators back in 1976. Autoerotic asphyxiation is allegedly a well-known practice of transvestites.

As a result of the circumstantial evidence of the botched and apparently hindered investigation by then chief of police Homer Davis, combined with lost evidence and the twelve years since the death of Pamela, Mark Whitfield was found not guilty of murder. The rape charges had been thrown out earlier due to the statute of limitations. Judge McMonagle said there was insufficient evidence to convict. The decision came on the ninth day of the trial and included a statement by the court that with the years between her dying and the trial some witnesses were left with a vague recollection of what happened.

The judge also made note that there was no question that evidence disappeared, was unaccounted for, and was destroyed. Whitfield stated after the verdict that he was pleased the ordeal was over and that he hoped Miss Terrill could finally rest in peace. Relatives of Pamela contended that she did not kill herself and was raped by Whitfield as claimed. But the judge made the decision and they would have to abide by it.

Citizens of Medina County were cheated out of two very important and emotionally needed closures. The first is from the years of controversy surrounding the death of a twenty-one-year-old young woman who was a resident, friend, coworker, and family member to the community. With the not-guilty verdict of the only suspect ever considered, Pamela's death will go unsolved.

The second important loss was that there was never an outcome of the special grand jury findings. After Whitfield's exoneration, the county closed the grand jury investigation. There could have been other criminal charges that would have emerged if they had been allowed to continue their investigation and make those findings open to the public—closure that would finally end all of the accusations and beliefs of corruption from the police department all the way up the ladder to the county commission and court system.

Retired judge Neil Whitfield died in a Florida nursing home in October of 1992. Over the course of his career as a judge, he was both commended for his knowledge of the law and remembered by his friends as fair and personable. He was probably the most powerful man in Medina County at one time. His time on the bench was marred by attempted citizen recalls and alleged rulings that made national headlines up to and including possible corruption in the investigation in the 1980s. He resigned abruptly in 1986 and moved to Florida with his wife.

Howard Servens, a friend of the judge who only knew him outside of the legal profession, said that the judge was a "man of principle, and if he believed something, he did it."

Mark Whitfield still seemed to have legal problems, even after being found not guilty of killing Pamela Terrill. In February of 1995, the Medina County Sheriff's Department opened an investigation into a January 2, 1995, fire at the bar and restaurant Boogies, property he and his wife owned.

There was an estimated $250,000 in damage, and it appeared from reports the fire was started by gasoline and ruled "arson" by investigators. This arson was the first one in Westfield Township since 1979.

The Whitfields had leased the bar to Thomas Bogdan, who also wanted to buy the building. According to an article in the *Akron Beacon* on February 3, 1995, Bogdan stated, "This is pretty hard to take because we ran a pretty good business. We had no trouble with any of our customers. In the year and a half I owned it, we only had one minor incident."

Bogdan said he had worked hard to build the business back up after Whitfield's previous bar business, Chumbuddies, failed. The liquor permit transferred from Whitfield to Bogdan in March 1994. Bogdan said he had an agreement written into the lease that Whitfield was not allowed on the property without advance notice because of his notoriety. "A lot of people in this community just don't want to have much to do with him," Bogdan said of Mark Whitfield. "I just didn't want him on the property because it wasn't good for business."

Pamela's death has one-half of a silver lining that still cries out for not only justice in her own life being taken away but also for at least three other deaths that were believed to be suspicious enough that a special grand jury was impaneled to look into them. Findings that have not been released or resolved for:

Mrs. Marjorie Whitfield, Judge Whitfield's wife, allegedly died from an overdose of insulin and ruled a suicide. According to records, Mrs. Whitfield was not a diabetic. An investigation into her death was allegedly halted thirty years ago. What were the results of her grand jury inquiries? Why would she commit suicide? And if that were true, was there a note?

Mr. Charles A. Witenhafer was bludgeoned to death in the basement of his home in 1980. What was the grand jury's evidence that they were looking at?

Mr. Harry L. Sugden was a forty-eight-year-old International Salt company employee from Michigan who was found dead in a motel on January 30, 1977. His death was ruled a suicide even though County Coroner Andrew Karson did not perform an autopsy or other tests to come to that conclusion. What were the facts surrounding his death that interested the grand jury?

What did the grand jury learn about the cover-ups and other alleged injustices they were investigating? And why have those findings never been brought to the public's knowledge?

Pamela Terrill's death should have a legacy and meaning besides just being another unsolved murder of a young girl who was buried in an unmarked grave. She could be remembered in Medina, Ohio's history as the one person who in death was successful in bringing a halt to all of the alleged corruption, injustice, and turmoil that occurred for years—the single person who embodied a whole county to finally want changes and make positive strides to become what it is today. If it wasn't for this person's life being taken away, none of this could have happened as it did.

Is it possible now in 2007 that the federal government could investigate the death of Pamela Terrill and the other events that occurred in Medina County as a violation of civil rights and government corruption? It's not uncommon for the FBI in this day and age to go back in past decades to do so. Would it not be a federal rights violation if she were killed to either cover up Elected Commissioner Mark Whitfield's sexual assault or other illegal or unethical acts she knew about him and others?

What about the other two unresolved murders of Harry L. Sugden and Charles A. Witenhafer allegedly to cover up government or political corruption? Could Marjorie Whitfield have known something she shouldn't have? These are unanswered questions that the U.S. Attorney could finally put to rest.

Police still ask for your help with these mysterious death cases. They have said not to discount the relevance of any information you may know. Your piece of information may have a significant impact on the investigation when viewed in the context of what they already know.

For further information, contact the Medina County Sheriff's Department at 330-725-9116, or you can E-mail Unsolvedmurder07@aol. com, and we will pass along this information.

Research and development of this story was made possible by the assistance of the Reference Department of the Akron-Summit County Public Library, friends and family of Pamela Terrill, and the Medina City Police and Sheriff's Department records.

Who Killed Ramona Krotine?

Had Jeffrey Krotine been playing baseball and had three strikes against him, he would have been called out. Being tried by a jury three times for murdering his wife was not a game he could afford to lose. Krotine, once a State Farm Insurance manager in Ohio, enjoyed making up to $325,000 a year and the lifestyle that accompanied the salary. Now his home, savings, and any plan for a luxurious retirement have gone up in smoke along with his former career.

Fifty-three-year-old Ramona Krotine, pictured to the right, was seen leaving a party in the early morning hours of March 21, 2003. The gathering was held at the Clarion Hotel on Bagley Road in Middleburg Heights. Mrs. Krotine met with some friends and others from the Sportsman Show being held  at the Cleveland Convention Center. Ramona reportedly left around 2:30 a.m. and headed towards her Toyota Camry. Mel Twinning stated he saw her at the party. Then later, while he had gone outside for a cigarette, he noticed a commotion over by a Camry around 2:30 a.m.

Twinning also described seeing a man standing by the car while it appeared another person was struggling with something or someone in the back seat. He later stated he thought it could be someone holding another person down. Paula Smith, another of Ramona's friends at the party, stated, "I heard a bang." There are reports that a coworker of Mrs. Krotine's, Susan Ziegler, said she had found a bizarre voicemail message on her answering machine that came in at 6:45 a.m. after the party with an eerie voice of a woman pleading for help before the call went dead.

One person seen dancing with Ramona the night she disappeared was a convicted thief. A witness, the man's coworker, decided to leave and go home but first offered the man a ride since he always rode public transportation. He refused a free ride, so the witness left. The next day, the same person showed up for work allegedly with long scratches on his hands and head, stating he had been mugged. The witness did not think anything about it until he learned of Ramona's disappearance and the events surrounding the discovery of her body, specifically where she was found. The witness stated he never cared much for his coworker and that he was a "con-man" with a felony record for theft.

When she did not return home Friday morning, Ramona's brother Greg set out to find his missing sister. Later that night, he came across her car in the parking lot of the Brookpark Road rapid transit station. All of the car doors were locked, but he noticed a small amount of blood on the passenger door handle. After smashing out the window, he discovered more blood in the back seat. Releasing the trunk lid only confirmed the fear that had overtaken Ramona's brother. Lying in the trunk was his sister's lifeless body (pictured 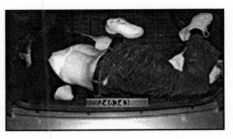 to the right), which had been beaten, bruised, and shot in the side of the head. Missing from her car was the large cash deposit due to go to the bank that day.

A few weeks later, police and prosecutors painted a different picture of what they say really happened—a theory that led to the arrest of her husband, Jeffrey Krotine (pictured below), months later. In the beginning, even law enforcement thought it was a murder-robbery. But after Jeff Krotine made several remodeling changes in his home days after the killing, they quickly targeted him as the alleged murderer.

 Prosecutors contend that Ramona made it home that night and a terrible fight ensued between husband and wife. Enough so that Jeff became very violent and continuously slammed her head into the wooden bed board until she was unconscious. He then allegedly carried the body wrapped in sheets or a blanket to the garage, then shot her in the head with his 9 mm pistol and drove to the rapid transit station, where he abandoned both his wife and the car. Blood droplets were found in the house in several places. The DNA did match Ramona's, but Jeff's lawyer contends that living in a house for twenty-five years it's probable at some point in time you are going to get a cut or scratch and bleed.

Family, friends, and neighbors were suspicious of the renovations made to the bedroom and other parts of the home shortly after the funeral. Spending $2,500 to have "spring cleaning" also seemed a bit much—unless one is trying to hide something. Another question that was haunting law enforcement was how unconcerned he appeared when his wife allegedly had not come home that night. He went to work like nothing was wrong even though his wife may have been missing.

Within ten months of the murder, a warrant was issued for Jeff Krotine and he turned himself in to police in February of 2004. The prosecution contended their case was based on circumstantial evidence but it would be more than enough to show that Krotine murdered his wife. Along with all of the other clues came the bombshell that Jeff had been having an affair for two years with Mary Engel, who worked in his office. Krotine admitted to the long-term relationship and believed his wife was unaware.

The first and second trial ended in mistrials when the jury could not come to a unanimous decision. On the third trial, Jeff Krotine was found not guilty.

The defense was able to poke holes through the prosecution's circumstantial theories. If Jeff drove the car to the transit depot station, how did he get eight miles back to their home? Daughter Jennifer Krotine was at home on school break and contends she never heard any arguing, fighting, or loud noises from her parents' bedroom, which was very close to hers. In fact, Jennifer alleges she was in their room early the next morning sitting on the bed and even did sit-ups on the bedroom floor. Nothing looked wrong, damaged, or out of place to her.

Jeff had answers for questions about carpet being taken up and the other remodeling to the home. As suspicious as it may have appeared, it wasn't proof that he murdered his wife. He also explained his behavior of going to work the morning Ramona did not come home. Both Jeff and their daughter stated these parties could get pretty wild and he thought his wife had more than likely stayed over at a coworker's house. Statements made by family and friends painted a picture of the marriage as not being close. After the kids were grown and out of the house, Jeff spent most of his time at work or out on the lake. Ramona, on the other hand, was very outgoing and sociable. She had a part-time job and enjoyed being around others. Jeff freely admits he committed adultery, but not murder.

The defense attacked the police for not following up on the witness accounts of the struggle in the hotel's parking lot, the loud bang heard, and the blood on the door handle that they contend was not Jeff's or Ramona's. Then there is the voicemail tape of a woman begging for help. Why hadn't the police followed up on other possible suspects like the man who was seen dancing with her not long before she left? Jeff's lawyers accused the detectives of bungling the case and allowing the real killer to escape justice.

An alleged red fiber found on her body was lost. There were leaves on her back that had disappeared also. Witness Mel Twinning says he went to the police with what he saw and heard the night of the murder, describing the commotion and people over by a Toyota Camry in the parking lot. Twinning alleges that the prosecution knew what he had seen for over a year but they did not want to hear it, saying his information could hurt their case. "If they treat all their witnesses like me, it's no wonder no one testifies," he says. "I went down there to do some good and got treated terrible."

Krotine was offered a plea deal to a lesser charge by the prosecutor during the third trial. Instead of turning it down because he wasn't guilty, Jeff said that if he pled to the charge, the real killer would remain free. His own feelings of who, why, and where have led him to openly speculate a conspiracy theory that State Farm Insurance had it in for him because of a contract dispute and that they conspired within State Farm's corporate offices to hire a hit man to kill his wife.

Jeff states that his lawyer's private investigator knows the true identity of the killer. True or not, a jury of twelve people says Krotine is innocent, and if you believe the theory that she was killed leaving the hotel, there is evidence that suggests this is true. One fact hasn't changed; someone killed Ramona Krotine in the early morning hours of March 21, 2003. Accepting the belief she was attacked in the hotel parking lot, there are the witnesses who saw her leave and even a suspect to consider.

She was seen leaving the hotel at approximately 2:30 a.m., according to Mel Twinning, who states he was outside when he noticed a man standing over by a Toyota Camry and what appeared to be another person forcing something into the back seat. Another witness claims to have heard a "bang" about the same time. Had someone followed her from the Convention Center, knowing she had left there with a large bank deposit, and planned to rob her? Ramona was seen earlier dancing with a convicted thief.

Then there is the mysterious voicemail message of a woman crying for help that was cut off. When Ramona's brother went searching for his sister, he found her car at the rapid transit station. Is there a connection between that specific location and the man Ramona was seen dancing with? Could she have offered him a ride while they were dancing? This same person shows up to work later that morning with long scratches on his hands and face from allegedly being mugged after the party?

Several questions still remain unanswered. How did Ramona Krotine go from the black strapped heels she was seen wearing during the hotel party to white tennis shoes and black socks, which was what she was wearing when her brother found her body in the trunk of the Camry? Did she change shoes before leaving the hotel? Or did she actually make it home and Jeff made that crucial mistake of not knowing what shoes she had worn that day as the prosecution contends?

Then there is the question of why Jeff burned the headboard from his and Ramona's bed only days after her murder—the same headboard prosecutor's allege he beat her head against. His statement to authorities and in a CBS news interview was that he never wanted another woman in his dead wife's bed. However, he kept the mattress and bed frame.

They say a killer makes up to twenty-five mistakes when committing murder and overlooks five of those to get caught. Jeff Krotine was found innocent by a jury. He is a free man, which means someone else may have killed Ramona and is still out there.

Police still ask for your help with this murder case. They have said not to discount the relevance of any information you may know. Your piece of information may have a significant impact on the investigation when viewed in the context of what they already know.

For further information, contact the Brook Park Police Department at 216-433-1239, or you can E-mail Unsolvedmurder07@aol.com, and we will pass along this information.

Research and development of this story was made possible by the assistance of *Cleveland Scene Magazine*, friends and family of Ramona Krotine, Parma City police records, *Akron Beacon Journal*, and *Plain Dealer* newspaper.

as sheriff deputies were rescuing a hiker from nearby Jenner, California, they came upon the pair still in their side-by-side separate sleeping bags.

Jason and Lindsay had both been shot in the head at close range while they slept. Police determined the weapon was a .44 magnum lever action rifle or semi automatic.

Fish Head Beach was not easy to get to. It also was off-limits to people, but police knew couples would camp out down on the scenic view.

As police requested assistance from the FBI and other law enforcement agencies across the country, leads and suspects'

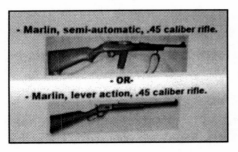

names quickly began to surface. One "person of interest" was Nicholas Edward Scarseth, a drifter from Wisconsin who was questioned and passed a polygraph exam and released.

Another suspect emerged whom police have been seeking for almost thirty-three years in connection with the murders of a young couple on Vancouver Island. Police have long sought Joseph Henry Burgess, described as a religious fanatic, because they believe he shot and killed Leif Carlsson and Ann Durrant, pictured to the right, as

they camped on a beach on Vancouver Island. They say his motive for killing the young couple was because they were cohabitating out of wedlock.

Investigators say Burgess waited for that couple to go to sleep and then shot them in the head with a .22 caliber rifle. Now police were looking for Burgess in the deaths of Lindsay

and Jason as well. The similarities were almost identical, which sent chills through the ranks of law enforcement. This man had possibly struck again and had been able to stroll around the United States freely to kill.

Police released this enhanced picture of what Burgess would look like today. Police say he is a religious fanatic. Burgess frequently quoted passages from the Bible, and cops say he closes his sentences with the word "Amen."

Police were also looking into similarities between their double homicide and a hauntingly similar murder that occurred

in Arizona a year earlier. In the Arizona case, Brandon Rumbaugh, twenty, and Lisa Gurrieri, nineteen (pictured to the left), two Scottsdale residents, were found at their campsite outside Bumble Bee, a ghost town in Yavapai County about an hour's drive north of Scottsdale on Interstate 17. Each had been shot in the head while sleeping in their sleeping bags, and there was no indication that they had been robbed or had struggled with their killer just as with Lindsay and Jason.

Rumbaugh was a student at Arizona State University and a member of the Marine Reserves who worked as a trainer in a local fitness center. Gurrieri was a business student at Mesa Community College in Mesa, Arizona, and sang in her local church choir. Like Cutshall and Allen, they were considered a model young couple.

Hundreds of people were interviewed over the course of the months after their murder, and the officers worked diligently tracking down each possible lead and suspect. Authorities wanted an effort to spark new leads and released some of the evidence retrieved at the crime scene. The sheriff's department released several pieces of crucial evidence they felt were pertinent in helping to solve this case.

Police want information on who drew these drawings of devil-like faces on driftwood that was located near the victims.

 This photograph of a necklace depicts one that was similar to what Lindsay Cutshall was reportedly given in the days leading up to the killing but was never located by detectives. This information is based upon statements from a witness in the case.

Authorities also released the sketch of a car they feel was in the area—a 1980s' or early 1990s' model, dark-colored sedan with tinted windows. The rear window has a black-and-white decal of a "crescent-shaped pollywog-like creature  with legs, such as something that could perhaps be referring to evolutionary theory," according to the Sonoma County Sheriff's Department. "One notable aspect of the decal is that it may be located closer to the center of the rear window than is typical."

Police also found this writing near the bodies of Jason and Lindsay with the very distinct "R" handwritten on the note.

A $60,000 reward is being offered for anyone who can provide information to the sheriff's department that leads to the arrest and conviction of those responsible. California Governor Schwarzenegger's Office posted $50,000 while a private party donated the other $10,000.

A memorial service was held to celebrate the lives of Lindsay Cutshall and Jason Allen at the Coshocton, Ohio's Church of the Nazarene in November of 2004. Fellow counselors who worked with both Lindsay and Jason recalled the selfless nature of the two faithful believers in God and their fellow man. Reverend Chris Cutshall, Lindsay's dad, felt blessed to have known Jason and thanked God that the two lived a life of selflessness and religious devotion. In prayer, he said, "We thank you for loving our kids and taking them home. God uses evil for good, and good will prevail."

Summing up their relationship, Pastor Cutshall recalled, "He didn't need a lot to be happy, and he found a girl who didn't need a lot to be happy." Lindsay had once written that she needed to live a less materialistic life and devote more of her time to her faith. She also wrote, "Live for things in heaven and not on earth." Her last writing on this earth while on the beach was "I look around and see creation all around me." Jason wrote, "God gives me the privilege in life, and he has given me a wonderful woman to enjoy it with."

Lindsay's and Jason's parents made a trip to California to visit the site where their children were murdered. They also made a plea to citizens not to give up on solving this crime, stating that just one lead passed along to the police could bring their killer to justice. Pastor Cutshall also made a plea to the person who killed his daughter:

"And to the killer himself ... you are out there somewhere, perhaps still in this area. We want you to know that you are not alone. God knows what you have done and He knows where you are and He will bring you to justice ... if not now, certainly at the Judgment, because you have innocent blood on your hands. As a pastor, as a servant of God, I want you to know that it would be better for you to turn yourself in and face justice now, and get help if you want it, and even forgiveness if you want that. It would be much better for you to turn yourself in than to continue to hide, but in the end, fall into the hands of the living God, which is a terrifying thing for a person like you. So we have come here today to offer you real grace ... an opportunity to come clean before it is eternally too late for you. We have come to ask you to turn yourself in."

Police still ask for your help with this double homicide. They have said not to discount the relevance of any information you may know. Your piece of information may have a significant impact on the investigation when viewed in the context of what they already know.

For further information, contact the Sonoma County Sheriff's Department at 707-565-2185, or you can E-mail Unsolvedmurder07@aol.com, and we will pass along this information.

Research and development of this story was made possible by the assistance of the Reference Department of the Akron-Summit County Public Library, *Coshocton Tribune*, friends and family of Lindsay and Jason, and the Sonoma County California Sheriff's Department records.

Who Killed Karen Michalski?

Karen Michalski wrote in a notebook shortly before her death in March of 1979, "If anything and I mean anything happens to me, do only one favor for me. Tell Bill I love him and I only wish things could have been different."

It would not be long after she wrote this that the tall brunette with long brown hair, blue eyes, and a warm smile for everyone was found slumped forward in her Oldsmobile with a shotgun blast to the back of her head. Sheriff's department employee Nora McNamara actually lived on Clifton Boulevard across from the Cynwood Apartments parking lot where the murder occurred. Nora reported hearing a loud bang, and looking out her window, she saw Michalski's car parked at an odd angle and a station wagon blocking it in.

Apartment resident Anne Jelson told investigators that she heard a horn blowing and a shot. Jelson told the *Plain Dealer* in a 1979 interview that she "heard the bangs and everything, and then this car sped away." Police may have had an eye witness to the minutes before Karen was killed.

Allegedly a truck driver called into the Lakewood police dispatcher a day later and claimed he had seen a dark-haired girl driving a 1974 to 1975 Oldsmobile and a man in a light-brown station wagon chasing her and bumping the back of her vehicle as they sped down the road near Detroit Road around 11:50 p.m. The trucker, who gave his name as "Redbird," described a man in a station wagon yelling at the female driver of the Olds something like "You'll pay for this." Redbird never revealed his true identity, and police were never able to successfully track the man down.

Detectives came up with several theories to her murder. Perhaps it was a deliberate execution at the hands of either someone she knew or someone who was hired to kill her. Or perhaps it was a random act of violence that escalated from a possible road rage incident. "Yet, senseless killings cannot be ruled out in our society," explained then assistant prosecuting attorney Sean Gallagher. Even reference to the notorious Drifters motorcycle club to a "murder for hire" plot was considered. Police say they investigated every two-bit thug or loser who fit any of the evidence at the time from their car, methods, prior records, and type of offense.

Captain Allen Clark stated in 1996 while he was reviewing the files and facts gathered to date that "the killer is in this report." Further he questioned the motive: "Was it jealousy; was it the eternal triangle?" Today Clark is retired from the police department. He found that he couldn't sit at home, so he accepted an offer to work as an investigator for the coroner's office. Clark readily admits he wishes he could have solved this murder before retiring, and he feels that he knows who the killer is.

"It bothers me a lot," then captain Clark explained to the reporter from the *Morning Journal* in Lorain. "It was an execution type slaying, one of the worst I have ever seen." Before his retirement, Clark wanted to make one last push. "I think solving this case would probably be the highlight of my career. To be able to take something that was so cold and get answers." Talking to the retired officer gave the impression he is still thinking about Karen's murder from time to time. And at least subconsciously, he waits for something to fall into place so he can call his detective comrades in Lakewood to catch the person responsible.

Wednesday night on March 7, 1979, found Karen meeting with friends for dinner and drinks. This outing had been planned since February when a former employee and friend from Boston was attending a science convention in Cleveland and asked if they could get together. Richard Tucker came to town as planned and met Karen at the Stouffers Inn. Both went to a hospitality suite in the hotel to meet other friends and left with a party of eleven people headed for Victoria Station in Rocky River. Three carloads of people traveled to the restaurant, one driver being Karen Michalski.

Michalski was described by her friends and family as always happy. A graduate from Lorain High School, Karen had many friends, some of whom were members of a ski club called "The Cast & Keg." One of fourteen children, she worked for a medical supply business and had aspirations of one day being an airline stewardess. Her older sister Sandi Kesterke reflects on her sister's murder, "Anytime I think about it today I still well up with tears." Saying also that her sister was a very loving and giving person with a lot of friends, she can't figure out why someone would want to hurt her.

That night in March of 1979 someone definitely wanted to hurt her. She was last seen by her dinner date and friends around 11:30 p.m. They remember that Karen seemed very relaxed and only had two Kahlua and Crème drinks and one glass of wine before the night's end. Detectives felt that she was chased by her killer in the station wagon and pulled into the first public place she could find that might have offered her help or at least drawn attention by blowing the horn.

They also thought that whoever shot the young woman appeared to have no set plan and possibly seized the moment when she stopped her car and he was able to block her in. Lakewood patrolman Ron Weidig was the officer who took the radio dispatch of the shooting. He immediately headed in the direction near Beach and Clifton, which was just a short time away from his location, but was delayed by a passing train. What he found when he arrived at the scene was the Cutlass with its engine still running. The glass on the driver's side of the car was shattered, and Karen was at the wheel slumped forward. She had been shot in the back of the head through the rear window at close range with a 16-gauge shotgun.

At one point during the initial investigation, it was said by some that they felt the police were handling the case too "gingerly" because one of the suspects had business dealings with the department. Others felt that the killer had insight into the schedules of the officers since her murder occurred during the evening shift change, during which only one patrol car was out in town. Detectives say there was nothing "gingerly" at all about the intense investigation into her murder.

Detectives have said that suspects were identified within the first three days, but they were never able to get the right piece of evidence to make a charge. Suspicion and motive gave investigators what they felt were two strong suspects. One was a coworker and the other was one of her friends from the ski club. Retired captain Clark said recently he still feels that this case can be solved. He also said that Detective Ginley, who now has the case file, is on the same page with Clark's gut feeling of who it is. When speaking to Ginley, the detective says the case is still open and he would love to be able to arrest and convict Karen's killer.

Police still ask for your help with this homicide. They have said not to discount the relevance of any information you may know. Your piece of information may have a significant impact on the investigation when viewed in the context of what they already know.

For further information, contact Detective Ginley of the Lakewood Police Department at 216-529-6767, or you can E-mail Unsolvedmurder07@aol.com, and we will pass along this information.

Research and development of this story was made possible by the assistance of the Akron-Summit County Public Library, *Plain Dealer* and *Akron Beacon Journal* newspapers, and friends and family of Karen Michalski.

Who Is the Deerfield Sniper?

In the early Saturday morning dark hours of November 6, 1993, Lisa Waters may have been sitting beside Andy Hussey on a fallen tree log on the Berlin Reservoir talking about her troubled past. They'd built a campfire inside a pit surrounded with rocks to keep the fire contained. Hussey, thirty-one, of Akron had been to the area many times fishing. His family also owned property nearby. Thirty-two-year-old Waters was from Kent, Ohio, and to date no one, not even their parents, knew that the two even knew each other.

As they sat talking, someone was watching them from up on a steep graded cliff sixty feet away. The couple below appeared a lot closer to the person peering down only because he was looking through the high-powered scope attached to his .30-30 caliber rifle. As the first round of the weapon sent a bullet into Andy Hussey's back, Lisa must have attempted to run as the person above chambered another round and took aim on her attempting to flee. Seconds later, another round was squeezed off, striking her in the back of the neck.

The coroner stated that both died instantly, so Andy had no idea of what hit him and Lisa had only seconds to realize something was terribly wrong. Two hunters found their bodies around 8:30 a.m. the same morning. They were fully dressed and lying where they had been killed. It was later ruled that the pair had been dead for approximately six hours. A few days later, as reporters interviewed Sheriff Duane Kaley, he stated that "whoever did this was a very good shot. They definitely knew what they were doing."

Police were going on the strong assumption that the killer was a longtime hunter and marksman. Others interviewed felt sure of the same theory and went one step further in saying that the weapon used was not legal to hunt with in the state of Ohio. Only .22 caliber rifles were allowed and that was for groundhog, pheasant, and rabbit shooting, which are usually daylight hunting. Interviewed by the *Akron Beacon Journal* in 1993, one avid hunter said, "The guy had to be a deer hunter and he had to have at least 3 to 4 years experience with that gun to fire, reload and fire again in the darkness while compensating for the steep download angle."

The murderer was quickly becoming known as the "Sniper," and police had no motive or suspects to link to the killer. Residents though made mention that the person could have been a deer poacher who felt since it was the beginning of rabbit and pheasant season the sound of gunfire would not be unusual. He may have changed his desire of prey from poaching deer to humans.

Lisa had led a troubled life and was said to have been diagnosed with having a chemical imbalance. She also had been through a turbulent marriage to Michael Schoolcraft, who had been charged in July of 1993 with allegedly raping her after they separated. He also had been charged four times for criminal trespassing and in 1992 for domestic violence. Court records also show that her former husband was found guilty in 1991 of child endangering when he used scalding hot water to bathe Lisa's then one-year-old son. The mother of three children had recently moved to the Akron area to try to rebuild her life. A check of Lisa's police report up until her death in 1993 only reveals a September 1993 charge of disorderly and public intoxication.

Less than a year later, in August of 1994, the body of a seventeen-year-old Alliance girl was found in the Berlin Reservoir area also. Kathryn Menendez had been strangled to death and sexually assaulted. When her body was first discovered, investigators could not tell if she had been shot, stabbed, or beaten. Her nude body was found by a gas company employee who was working in the area. Police and the coroner's office said it appeared the teenager had been tortured. It was also unknown if Kathryn had been killed where she was found or somewhere else then dumped where she was discovered.

Janet Menendez had reported her daughter missing days earlier, and other reports indicate Kathryn had been a habitual runaway for some time.

Less than three months later, the body of an unidentified teenage girl was found only a few hundred feet away from where Lisa's and Andy's bodies were discovered murdered in 1993. Her body was badly decomposed, and law enforcement had a difficult time making her identification. Sheriff Kaley said the Cuyahoga County Coroner's Office in Cleveland did determine that the body was a white female, between fourteen and eighteen years old, with strawberry-blond hair and a small to medium build, and was five feet to five feet two inches tall.

Her identity would later be solved by the initial excellent police work of Portage County Detective Cindy Balog in 1998,

who first noticed a missing person's flyer from Beaver County, Pennsylvania, and contacted authorities there.

But it would be in 2003 before positive identification could be made of the remains of fourteen-year-old Sarah Ray Boehm, pictured to the left. The positive ID was made through DNA by the FBI. When her body was discovered, police were trying to learn then if the little girl's body was in any way connected to Andy and Lisa in 1993.

Sarah had been reported missing by her mother, who lived in Rochester Township. She had left a note for her mother saying she was spending the night at a friend's house but never returned home. Mrs. Boehm remembers of her daughter: "She was a doll. She was sweet and a good student and beautiful." Her mother went on to say that Sarah was a cheerleader and would have been in the ninth grade the coming school year she disappeared.

The murders of Andy Hussey, Lisa Waters, Kathryn Menendez, and Sarah Boehm are still unsolved today.

Police still ask for your help with these four unsolved murders. They have said not to discount the relevance of any information you may know. Your piece of information may have a significant impact on the investigation when viewed in the context of what they already know.

For further information, contact the Portage County Sheriff's Department at 330-297-3890, or you can E-mail Unsolvedmurder07@aol.com, and we will pass along this information.

Research and development of this story was made possible by the assistance of the Reference Department of the Akron-Summit County Public Library, *Akron Beacon Journal*, friends and family of the victims, and police records from the Akron-Kent and Portage County Sheriff's Department.

Whose Ghost Stalks the Halls of Cleveland Justice?

Thirty years ago, the Criminal Courts Building in Cleveland was abandoned for the newer twenty-three-story Justice Center on Ontario Street. Cleveland was given a one-hundred-year lease on the old building if it promised to pay $1 a year. The old courthouse has been described as a "rough and tumble newsboy" according to a 1994 story by the *Plain Dealer.* "A hawker shouting out the latest crime news on the street corner." The closing of this older courthouse also sealed forty years of crime, corruption, and every conceivable civil and criminal case imaginable. From the halls of the twelve-story sandstone building on East Twenty-first Street, only two things can be heard or seen in the haunting years left behind: the ghosts of the unsolved murders still walking the halls searching for justice; and the sights and sounds of a new group of lawyers arguing divorce cases now being handled from this old courthouse building.

Prior to the city's current use for divorce cases, the building had remained vacant. Plaster dust coated the terrazzo floor.

Empty bottles of cheap wine littered the ledges and perched on the oak banisters of the witness stands. Ice glistened on the walls. Windows were open, allowing pigeons to fly in and out at will. The once-grand rotunda became a repository for the waste of vagrants. The words "kangaroo court" could be seen on the walls of Courtroom 3, perhaps a present-day testament to the acts of justice and injustice alike that were dealt out there not so long ago.

The courthouse opened its doors during a time when Eliot Ness was fighting prohibition. Machine-gun killings and corrupt city officials and crooked cops were at their height. Crime was mostly unstoppable, overflowing the county dungeon like a jail on Public Square, which was later replaced with this larger Criminal Courts Building.

One of Cleveland's councilmen, William E. Potter, was reportedly a feisty man, thus making him a well-known politician in town with stories about his questionable adventures that frequently landed him in the newspapers. At first, the articles were on how the former bricklayer fought for his district's voters. However, he was better known, through the media's attention, for his unethical habits and getting indicted over land deals.

On February 8, 1931, the day after the new Criminal Courts Building opened and the day before flamboyant Potter was to appear there on a perjury charge, he was found shot to death in his apartment. Allegedly he was to spill his guts about political colleagues and questionable land deals. It appeared someone didn't want him to talk. Was his murder just a coincidence, or had Potter been killed to shut him up? A reward of $21,000 was posted for information leading to his killer. Looking for the big break, detectives found a big one.

An overweight blond prostitute named Betty Gray was brought in for questioning. Gray lived in the Parkwood Drive building where Potter's body was found. She told police she had seen a suspicious-looking character in the building the day Bill was killed. She identified Hymen Martin, a bootlegger from Pittsburgh. Police went to Pennsylvania and arrested Martin. The media quickly named him "Pittsburgh Hymie." Martin, twenty-eight, was a sharp dresser whose dark hair fell over his forehead, and he would go down in history as the Criminal Courts Building's first celebrity.

His codefendant was his girlfriend, Mary Outland, nicknamed "Akron Mary" after her hometown. Police brought her from Pittsburgh too, and it was rumored she was being held as a material witness. Outland, a buxom brunette, didn't seem to mind her captivity. She was ready to testify that she was with her man the night of Potter's murder. Outland played it up to all of the media attention. Reports had her wearing a black turban, a pearl choker, and a black velvet dress as she seductively posed for photographers. "I wouldn't pose at all," she blurted from on top of one of the jail's desks, telling everyone she would never have posed like that except she wanted "my Hymie" to have a good picture of her.

Reporter Thiess in her 1994 story quoted a former writer from that time era that eluded to Outland not being opposed to having other men with a good picture of her as well. Webster Seeley, a Cleveland news reporter, allegedly told envious fellow reporters that he had bought a jail matron a quart of bootleg hooch in exchange for a private interview with Outland. According to the then reporter, who said "I walked into the cell and she was completely naked, giving herself a sponge bath," Seeley recalled, "She sat there like a queen, covering herself with a washrag, and answered all my questions. I had trouble remembering the questions, let alone the answers, but I had a Page One exclusive the next day."

The day before Martin's trial was to begin, hundreds of men gathered about on the courthouse steps, seeking a spot in the courtroom. The trial opened on March 25, 1931, before Common Pleas Judge Walter McMahon. Allegedly one thousand spectators had been turned away for the one-hundred-seat courtroom. Those who managed to get seats varied from politicians to racketeers to several curious women who wanted a glimpse of the suave and handsome defendant Martin.

He hired one of the city's most famed attorneys, William E. Minshall. Minshall's opening statement was telling the jury that Martin was the victim of a frame up, that he didn't know Potter and had no reason to kill him. Prosecutor Ray T. Miller, the Democratic county prosecutor, admitted that the evidence against Martin was circumstantial but stated that Martin was hired by someone in Cleveland to kill Potter and had even rented "Hymie" the apartment in Potter's building.

The trial lasted one week. The day that Outland testified, the crowd almost broke down the courtroom doors. She smiled at Martin then cried. His eyes were never removed from hers as she testified about how they were driving from Cleveland to Akron at the time Potter was killed. The highlight of the trial came during Miller's summation to the jury. Miller had the bailiffs drag the small sofa that Potter was killed on into the courtroom. Miller put on Potter's blood-stained hat and fell onto the couch as the councilman must have when shot. "You cruelly shot that man in the back!" he yelled at Martin.

The jury bought it, finding Pittsburgh Hymie guilty. They did recommend mercy, which kept him from the chair. The court of appeals overturned the conviction a year later, saying Martin had not received a fair trial but one surrounded with "inflammatory vituperation." Martin was retried, but this time

Betty Gray changed her testimony saying she was not sure that Hymie Martin was the man she had seen the day Potter was killed.

Martin returned to Pittsburgh leaving Potter's murder still unsolved. Akron Mary stayed behind in Ohio, where she became the mistress of a prominent Cleveland man and lived in an apartment he provided for her. The death of William E. Potter remains an unsolved murder.

Also in the halls of justice was the legendary trial of Bay Village's Dr. Sam Sheppard, who put on a show of one of the most fantastic legal events the Criminal Courts Building had ever produced. Sheppard was charged with his beautiful wife's murder, and reporters from as far away as Australia flocked to hear his story told. Nearly half of the country's news industry put the trial's daily episodes on their front pages. The details of this case have since become books and TV movies. One incident reported by *Plain Dealer* reporter Doris O'Donnell writes like a scene out of a movie: "At one point during the trial, it was clear the jury would convict Sheppard, whom they had already learned was having an affair with his lab assistant."

But the prosecutor was not content with his apparent victory. He wheeled into the courtroom a covered wax model of Mrs. Sheppard's head, shaved to show the twenty-seven blunt instrument wounds made by her attacker. "It was pink, the color of her skin," O'Donnell recalls today. "They brought it into the courtroom covered with a cloth. When they took it off, I swear, for a moment everyone thought it was actually Marilyn's head." The jury found the doctor guilty of second-degree murder, and he was sent to the Ohio Penitentiary in Columbus.

In 1966, the U.S. Supreme Court ruled that his 1954 trial had been nothing more than a "carnival atmosphere" and reversed the conviction. Sheppard was retried and this time was acquitted. He went on to marry twice more and, according to his wives, found peace and comfort in drinking and drugs. He died in April 1970 in Youngstown, Ohio, where he had moved. His legacy would be in TV episodes of *The Fugitive*. That would also become a movie starring Harrison Ford as the doctor. The death of Marilyn Sheppard remains an unsolved murder.

Over the years, good and bad guys would walk through the doors of the Criminal Courts Building seeking some form of justice. Overshadowed by corruption among politicians, prostitution, or an occasional murder in downtown Cleveland, the residents had thought they'd seen it all. But murder had found its way to the suburbs. Hazel Gogan was murdered in her Lakewood home in 1950. This case had all the ingredients for a movie. Mrs. Gogan, forty-seven, was a heavyset brunette known for her expensive jewelry and clothing.

She had a collection of diamond rings, earrings, and necklaces valued at approximately $140,000, which her husband, Joseph Gogan, had lovingly presented to his wife in the happier days of their marriage. Joseph, sixty-three, was a wealthy businessman who owned the Gogan Machine Shop in Cleveland.

Mr. Gogan ended up on the wrong side of the law and another side of living conditions, which included a tiny cell in the basement of the Criminal Courts Building. The Gogans' happy marriage had gone south during the summer of 1948, when Mrs. Gogan found out from her husband he had spent a night with another woman in a stateroom on a boat while cruising Lake Erie. Hazel was furious and told her husband she wanted a separation and divorce. He agreed and moved into his estate in Kirtland while she stayed in their Clifton Boulevard home.

A two-year separation didn't ease the tension between them at all. In 1950, they began arguing over anything, such as who would keep the three portraits by the Italian painter G. Magno Firenze. Paintings by other artists included one of Hazel and one of Joseph and even one of a family scene. Hazel told her husband he was free to take his own likeness with him since she had gotten tired of seeing his face on the wall. The other two would stay with her.

On July 17, while Hazel was on the telephone with a friend, Joseph broke out the front window to get into the house he hadn't lived in for two years. He would later tell police he went there to get some garden tools and some rat poison (cyanide), which he planned to use out at his Kirtland farm. The argument with his wife over the portraits started again. One thing led to another, and the next thing he knew, Joseph said, Hazel was screaming and struggling with him. The bag of cyanide that Joseph was carrying broke, creating a cloud of powder.

Joseph claimed that as he was leaving the house, his wife walked toward the rear of their home apparently to wash the powder from her face.

Police were called to the house by a neighbor after Joseph left. They discovered the living room reeking with the sickening fumes of cyanide and Hazel lying on the sofa semi-unconscious with her tongue hanging from her mouth. Police noticed her face was spotted and covered with a white powder. They took her to Lakewood Hospital, where she died two hours later. An autopsy showed that death came as a result of her inhaling the cyanide powder. Cuyahoga County Coroner Samuel Gerber said the rat poison had created a "lethal gas chamber" around Hazel.

Joseph Gogan was arrested the next day after police found out that he would inherit $225,000 from his wife's insurance policy. At first he told police he smacked Hazel in the face with the bag of powder and then later changed his story to say that some of the powder must have gotten on Hazel's face after the bag broke during their fight. The trial in the Criminal Courts Building began on December 4, 1950, with attorneys William J. Corrigan and Fred Garmone representing Mr. Gogan. While the state tried to prove murder, Gogan and his defense attorneys claimed Hazel suffered a heart attack after the struggle.

Onlookers packed the courtroom again just like with the murder trial of Councilman Potter. This trial would last seven weeks, giving almost everyone a chance to watch the case evolve. The evidence turned on the credibility of the prosecution's tests used to determine if cyanide was present in human tissue. The tests were new and controversial, and the jury appeared confused. Then a *Cleveland Press* reporter stunned everyone when he turned up a witness to the alleged crime: a Boston terrier named Mitzi. Reporter Bus Bergen overheard one day at the trial that Mitzi was Hazel's dog that was always at her side. In fact, the dog was guarding her when police arrived at the home.

There had been no mention of Mitzi during the trial. But Bergen checked with some doctors who told him that a ten-pound dog would be killed by cyanide fumes long before a 160-pound woman. Defense attorneys, previously unaware of the dog, jumped on the information and found medical experts who testified to the same thing. If enough cyanide had been released to kill Mrs. Gogan, it would have killed Mitzi too. Since it hadn't, Mrs. Gogan should have been unaffected by the poison and most likely did die of a heart attack.

The jury agreed with the defense. Joseph Gogan was acquitted. He allegedly hugged Mitzi to him as he walked through the hallways of the Criminal Courts Building a free man. Old Mitzi helped save Joe's life. He chortled as he scratched her head. "How glad we are to meet again, Mitzi girl, my girl." Within a week of his acquittal, Joseph Gogan reported receiving more than 150 letters from female admirers who wanted to marry. But Gogan married the woman from Pennsylvania, and he took great care of Mitzi until the end of her days.

The Criminal Courts Building was not just a hangout for corruption and criminals. Racism was rampant in not only the city in the 1950s but in the court system as well. Cleveland's few black lawyers found a system that devised many ways to lock them out. During the 1950s, it was still an open practice by the town's major law firms not to hire black attorneys. The majority of downtown buildings refused to even rent office space to black lawyers.

Cleveland's big-shot lawyers went after the high-profile and profitable civil and corporate cases. Criminal defense wasn't paying any money, so they had little time for it. Lawyers were paid a flat fee to defend a client who couldn't afford a private attorney no matter how much time the lawyer put in. Dealing with the indigent clients who found themselves in trouble in criminal court hardly made it worth their effort.

Less fortunate lawyers, those not employed by the large firms, had to take on the court-appointed cases just to make a living. Since there was no public defender's office then, there was plenty of work to go around defending the hundreds of people who came through the county's justice system each year.

Stanley E. Tolliver was a black lawyer who got his start doing criminal work on East Twenty-first Street. "That courthouse was a boon to black lawyers," he says. "We'd all run into each other every day, and the older lawyers would help the young lawyers." There was a real spirit of brotherhood. "I don't think I've ever seen anything like it since." The black group consisted of Merle McCurdy, who would later become the first black U.S. district attorney; Carl Stokes, who would become Cleveland's mayor; his brother Lou Stokes, a future congressman; Norman S. Minor; Granville Bradley; and Charles Fleming.

They actually formed a club that was part professional, part social, and called it the "John M. Harlan Club" in honor of the U.S. Supreme Court justice who argued so passionately against racial discrimination. The Harlan Club members would spend hours discussing politics over the meals served at Rosie's, a soul food restaurant across from the courthouse.

It wasn't until the 1960s that the black lawyers' fraternity really gained some momentum. Judges running for election began approaching them for help in getting votes from black voters who were quickly becoming the majority. The lawyers were pleased to get involved. Going door to door in their neighborhoods to get out the vote and talking up the judges at community meetings, they hoped that in return the judges would increase the number of clients they sent their way. And it worked.

"It used to be that even black defendants wanted Jewish lawyers, because a lot of the judges were Jewish and they thought that would help them," Tolliver says. "But as black judges began to be elected, and black lawyers were getting a good reputation, defendants began asking for us." And an occasional high-profile case captured some publicity for the black lawyers, if not always the money their white counterparts earned. "The big-shot lawyers looked down on us," Tolliver says. "But sometimes they were jealous, too. So I'd tell 'em, 'You got the fortune, we got the fame.'"

Fred Evans, a Black Nationalist organizer accused of starting the bloody Glenville riot in 1968, was charged with the murder of three Cleveland policemen and a civilian during the rioting. Attorneys Tolliver and Fleming agreed to represent him at trial. Fred Evans had changed his name to Ahmed after joining the Islamic faith and made his living from a storefront astrology parlor on Superior Avenue near Lakeview Road.

Evans was militant, and his beliefs were fueled by the passive resistance philosophy of the Rev. Dr. Martin Luther King, Jr. But when King was assassinated in April 1968, any passivity Evans harbored changed to outrage. "The Beast (white man) killed the best friend it ever had when it killed Martin Luther King," Evans said. "There is no hope for me now." He urged his followers in the Glenville neighborhood to prepare for violence.

On the night of July 23, 1968, Evans, wearing a beret and dashiki and his carbine over his shoulder, took to the streets with other followers who joined him. The militants surrounded two city tow truck drivers trying to tow an illegally parked car on Beulah Avenue. One driver was shot in the leg. Gunfire began all around as locals poured out of their homes and police took over the area.

By the next morning, three of Evans' militant friends were dead. So were three policemen and six civilians. When Evans was arrested that day, he allegedly told police, "My men died for a good cause." Charged with seven counts of first-degree murder, he was jailed and awaiting trial. Many in the black community felt Evans had been railroaded by a system that favored whites. Protesters moved to the Criminal Courts Building, which they felt symbolized oppression by the law.

Before Evans' trial began, a group of several dozen demonstrators tried to get into Prosecutor John T. Corrigan's office to talk to him about alleged unfairness to blacks in the justice system. Corrigan refused to see them. A few days later, a court order was issued to keep the protesters out of the building's hallways.

Willie Mae Mallory was one of the group's leaders who was barred from entering. "This is an order against all blacks," she shouted. "Okay ... block it off!" she commanded, motioning the others to blockade the double doors. A scuffle quickly broke out on the front steps. A court employee's mouth was bloodied in the outbreak, which drew twenty helmeted deputy sheriffs out of the building to arrest twenty-five protesters, including Mallory.

Throughout the trial, the protests continued in front of the courthouse. When the all-white jury found Evans guilty, he was sentenced to spend the rest of his life behind bars. Deputies feared another riot was about to break out, so they snuck Evans out the back of the building and into an awaiting helicopter that flew him to the Ohio Penitentiary in Columbus. He was gone before his lawyers or anyone else knew it. Evans died ten years later in a Columbus hospital from cancer.

As the Criminal Courts Building's legacy and doors were closing for good in 1970, authorities realized it couldn't come quick enough to head off one of the most memorable escapes in Ohio's history. On March 27, 1970, three prisoners kidnapped two elderly ladies, Norina Dellaria, sixty-two, and Louise Honour, seventy-one. Both were members of the Christian Scientist Church who had been visiting the jail for five years to lead services. Somehow, federal prisoners Thomas E. Thomas and James Snyder, who had already escaped from a Mississippi prison, along with David E. Carpenter, held for forging an auto title, got their hands on a toy gun and some very real knives.

The prisoners grabbed the two women and made their way to the building's basement. Cuyahoga County Sheriff Ralph Kreiger agreed to give them a Warrensville Heights police car so they could escape. Kreiger also had a deputy sheriff give them a shotgun with one shell in it. The car sped away as it headed through downtown toward Interstate 71. Back at the jail, deputy sheriffs and police jumped in their cars to give chase. The pursuit would take them to Kentucky.

The prisoners drove down I-71 and were chased by police from nearly every community they passed through. Forty police cars made a long caravan flying down the interstate. The convoy concluded when the inmates encountered a Kentucky state trooper who decided to put an end to the flashing light parade. Near Lexington, Kentucky, and still in his patrol car, he took careful aim at the escapees' car tires and shot them out. The prisoners came out with their hands up, and Dellaria and Honour, who were quite shaken and exhausted, were helped out of the car. They hadn't been harmed. They claimed their faith had protected them.

The Criminal Courts Building itself was locked up in 1976, leaving inside the years of legitimate and blind justice, along with the stories that could be told for generations to come.

Research and development was aided by the Cleveland *Plain Dealer*, Cleveland Public Library, and the Cleveland Restoration Society.

About the Author

Jack Swint is fifty-three years old, married, and works in the news media industry in Ohio. His resume reads like his first published novel, *Creative Impulse,* in which Jack details his own personal life of impulsive behavior that has landed him on both sides of the law—a life that has also placed him face to face with celebrities, politicians, and famous criminals across the country while working for the government and also as an investigative consultant for Fox TV's *A Current Affair.* There is nothing though on his resume or in his personal life that could have prepared him for investigating then writing this first series of "Who Killed …?" Everyone has seen death before, but these are cases of brutal, malicious, and sadistic acts of cold-blooded murder inflicted on both adults and children. Utilizing a writing style that has been called "terse with few wasted words," Jack quickly deletes most of the melodrama and goes straight for the truth and facts of each unsolved murder.

Printed in the United States
76248LV00001BB/205-1248